LEADER'S MANUAL

# VACATIONS WITH A PURPOSE

## A Planning Handbook
## for Your Short-Term Missions Team

### CHRIS EATON AND KIM HURST

**SINGLES MINISTRY RESOURCES**

NAVPRESS

A MINISTRY OF THE NAVIGATORS
P.O. BOX 35001, COLORADO SPRINGS, COLORADO 80935

The Navigators is an international Christian organization. Jesus Christ gave His followers the Great Commission to go and make disciples (Matthew 28:19). The aim of The Navigators is to help fulfill that commission by multiplying laborers for Christ in every nation.

NavPress is the publishing ministry of The Navigators. NavPress publications are tools to help Christians grow. Although publications alone cannot make disciples or change lives, they can help believers learn biblical discipleship, and apply what they learn to their lives and ministries.

Library of Congress Catalog Card Number: 90-63219
ISBN 08910-96094

Second printing, 1992

Cover photography: Mike Marshall

The song "I Love You, Lord" on page 127 is reprinted with the permission of Marantha! Music, Laguna Hills, California.

Thanks to those who contributed: Adele Calhoun, Jean Stephens, and Steve Webb.

Unless otherwise identified, all Scripture in this publication is from the *Holy Bible: New International Version* (NIV). Copyright © 1973, 1978, 1984, International Bible Society. Used by permission of Zondervan Bible Publishers. Other versions used include: the *Good News Bible: Today's English Version* (TEV), copyright © American Bible Society 1966, 1971, 1976; the *New American Standard Bible* (NASB), © The Lockman Foundation 1960, 1962, 1963, 1968, 1971, 1972, 1973, 1975, 1977; and the *King James Version* (KJV).

Printed in the United States of America

FOR A FREE CATALOG OF
NAVPRESS BOOKS & BIBLE STUDIES,
CALL TOLL FREE 1-800-366-7788 (USA)
or 1-416-499-4615 (CANADA)

# CONTENTS

*To Carey Caldwell and Rich Hurst,*

*who have played such significant roles in our lives,
our ministries, and our understanding of the process
and importance of short-term mission teams.*

# AUTHORS

**Chris Eaton** is president of Bridge Builders, Inc., a consulting group that assists churches in developing short-term mission teams and programs. Formerly, he was the executive director of Single Purpose Ministries, a decade-old, interdenominational singles ministry in Florida.

During his tenure with Single Purpose, Chris began developing curriculum to assist short-term teams. Over the past eight years he has facilitated numerous teams involving several hundred adults. He is also a frequent speaker at singles groups around the United States.

**Kim Hurst** is one of the founders and former coordinators of the Vacations with a Purpose program at the University Presbyterian Church in Seattle, Washington, a 3,500-member church.

The curriculum and program policies developed at University Presbyterian Church have been used successfully by many churches wanting to implement short-term mission teams.

Kim's interest in other cultures was stimulated by a period of travel as a member of Up With People. She has led numerous short-term mission teams and is currently finishing her masters degree in cross-cultural studies at Fuller Seminary. Kim and her husband, Rich, have one child.

# ACKNOWLEDGMENTS

This book, like the teams it describes, could not have existed without the prayers and hard work of many concerned people who helped us at every stage. We'd like to express our thanks to those who have contributed so much to the short-term mission programs at Single Purpose Ministries and University Presbyterian Church, to those who have encouraged and assisted us with this book. We are both indebted to Carey Caldwell and Rich Hurst who were partners with us at every step. Many of the ideas in this book (especially in chapters 9, 10, and 14) originated with them.

There were also many others who contributed to the experiences that we drew upon to write this book. At the risk of omitting some, we'd like to especially mention Jerry O'Leary, Bruce Larson, Art Beals, John Westfall, Rob Turner, Rob Phillips, Nancy Nielsen, Traci Anderson, Jeff Hussey, Jim Vasquez, Linda Menke Vasquez, Sandy Gwinn, Laurie Krinke, Jim Towry, Wanda Grewe, and the board of directors of Single Purpose Ministries, Inc. We'd also like to thank those who read and commented on the manuscript (even though we didn't heed all of your good advice, we sincerely appreciate it): Adele Calhoun, Park Street Church in Boston; Henry Williams, Westlink Christian Church in Wichita; Carey Caldwell, Bridge Builders, Inc., in St. Petersburg; Jerry O'Leary, University Presbyterian Church in Seattle; and Doug Millham, Discover The World, Inc., in Pasadena. Also, our thanks go to Jerry Jones for seeing the importance of this project and for giving us the much-needed encouragement to keep going and to meet our deadlines.

Finally, we wish to thank the scores of team leaders, team members, missionaries, and hosts whose lives have been interwoven through Vacations with a Purpose, and who provided the inspiration for this book.

# PART ONE

# WHAT'S BEHIND A VACATION WITH A PURPOSE?

# CHAPTER ONE

# WHAT IS A VACATION WITH A PURPOSE?

## VACATIONS WITH A PURPOSE

What comes to mind when you hear the term? You may react like most hard-working adults: Every vacation has a purpose—to get away from the job and take it easy. Some crave peace and quiet while others cannot wait to escape the humdrum of everyday living and embark on an adventure. They long to meet new and interesting people, travel to faraway places, feast on exotic dishes, and collect some good stories to take back to the office.

This book is for those who are ready to step beyond normal routines and quiet vacations into the exciting world of short-term missions. Vacations with a Purpose, or VWAPs (pronounced Vee-Waps), are short mission trips that give people the opportunity to meet new friends, live in community, experience a different culture and best of all, see God at work.

The phenomenal growth of short-term mission teams, or VWAPs, reflects our ever-shrinking world and our ever-growing appetite for inter-cultural exposure. Doug Millham, the founder of the church mobilization program called Discover the World, whose doctoral dissertation dealt with short-term missions, states that between 1979 and 1989 the numbers of people involved per year in short-term missions rose from just over 25,000 to approximately 120,000. Concurrently, the number of agencies involved with short-termers has grown from fifty to more than 400! Churches and parachurch organizations that offer such programs are besieged by requests from church leadership seeking information and assistance in developing programs of their own.

Mission agencies are also noticing that career-aged professionals (who can't imagine living abroad for even a few years) thrill at the opportunity to experience cross-cultural missions for their annual vacation. John Huffman, director of Latin American Missions' "Christ for the Cities" program (CFC), has gone so far as to say that "commuter missionaries" are the wave of the future. His organization has been greatly aided and encouraged by teams of properly prepared, energetic VWAPers who have traveled to CFC projects to serve, learn, and form relationships with their Latin brothers and sisters in Christ.

But the list of those who benefit through short-term mission teams extends beyond career missionaries and team participants. Local church pastors are discovering that their entire congregations are affected as well. The men, women, and youth who participate in such an experience begin to develop a greater maturity and become more effective church members. They, in turn, strengthen the whole church. Like many other ideas whose "time has come," the concept of fostering Christian discipleship among congregations through this type of cross-cultural involvement is one that many are realizing simultaneously.

An example of how this idea occurred to several people at once is found in our own stories. We didn't know each other in the early 1980s when we each had a part in "inventing" the short-term teams programs for our ministry groups, yet the programs we helped develop were almost identical.

## KIM'S STORY

Vacations with a Purpose began for me in 1985 at University Presbyterian Church (UPC) in Seattle. Two members of the UPC singles department commented on the beauty of their vacations to Mexico. But they felt frustrated that they had been unable to appreciate and know Mexico's finest asset—its people. Was there a way to get to know the people in a short vacation? What if UPC singles could spend their vacation with Mexican Christians? A group of six of us began to meet and pray about where we might begin.

Within months, the first UPC Vacations with a Purpose team was working in Mexico, hand in hand with missionaries and Mexicans. We intended to "better the lives" of orphaned and abandoned children as well as to aid the poor Indian migrant workers living close by. But as we offered our *hands* to the people we had gone to serve, we discovered something very profound occurring in our *hearts*. The smiles on the children's faces, the words of praise for God on the lips of the poorest field-workers, and the selflessness of the orphanage houseparents were all reaching out and changing us. We went to serve and returned to Seattle profoundly served.

Keeping in mind the word *vacation* in our title, we designed the schedule to conclude with a few days of rest and reflection at the beach in Ensenada. After the physically and emotionally draining days at the project site, we needed time for rest and perspective. Ensenada provided a psychological layover between the mission site and Seattle. Discussions at the meals and evening group meetings centered on making sure that our time in Mexico was not an isolated event. Would we let the experience change us? Would our personal philosophies and identities be marked forever by our venture into missions?

Since that first trip to Mexico, Vacations with a Purpose has expanded to include other countries, thus providing adults, both single and married, the opportunity to learn about God through the lives of Christians in many corners of the world. Team members have returned renewed, enlightened, and enthusiastic for ministry. Some have changed careers in midstream and become long-term missionaries. Others have become involved in church leadership as elders and teachers, or have participated in local ministries. Vacations with a Purpose is now one of the church's primary discipleship training tools and involves 300 adults from all sectors of the church. Members of the congregation who have never taken a Vacation with a Purpose have found their own outlook reshaped and their world enlarged through the experiences of former team members.

Our experiences, along with those of people in other churches, have taught us a great deal about what makes a team work. But more importantly, we have learned that there is no limit to the way God can reveal Himself to those who are willing to see Him through the eyes of another.

## CHRIS'S STORY

Ironically, my venture into VWAP began with a "failure." In 1983 several lay leaders in Single Purpose, a ministry for single adults in South Florida, expressed interest in "doing something" overseas, something that would fit into their vacation schedules. A trip lasting more than two weeks was out of the question, but a one-to-two-week trip was quite feasible.

A trip was scheduled to Haiti in conjunction with another agency. Planning, recruiting, and training all went smoothly. But then, one week before the team's departure, work plans in Haiti fell apart. I was left to decide whether or not to go through with the trip. I desperately wanted people to have the opportunity for this type of experience, but I did not want to waste the money that had been invested. In the end, I decided not to take the team to Haiti. But I resolved to take a team the following year and to be more purposeful in the planning.

In 1984 the first Single Purpose short-term mission team went to a school for the deaf outside Port-au-Prince, Haiti. That team began what has become our greatest tool for developing leadership, for discipling our members, and for launching people into ministry and mission. The feedback from host churches and mission agencies with whom we have worked has been overwhelming.

Since that first trip, Single Purpose has taken more than 300 people (the majority of whom were single) overseas as part of over twenty-five short-term projects. The teams, composed largely of unskilled laborers, have generally participated in work projects, ranging from building benches to constructing school buildings. All have worked in partnership with the nations from the particular countries. This sort of cooperation encourages meaningful interaction with the nationals and eliminates the perception that this is merely a "North American" project.

Our teams often construct buildings, but more importantly, the experience builds lives. After six years, I am still amazed to see how life-changing a one-or-two-week experience can be. As people work, worship, and live with others of a different culture, they learn much more about the other culture, and a great deal more about themselves.

When we met in 1987, we discovered our mutual enthusiasm for the benefits of short-term mission teams. We enjoyed comparing notes about travel hints, proper training, spiritual applications, etc. We also found that there were numerous church leaders who wanted to start programs like ours, and they were eager for any information we could provide.

Initially, we started writing this book with the desire to provide curriculum and training material for church leaders like those who had contacted us. However, as people became aware of our endeavor, we realized this was a resource needed by others as well. We spoke to missionaries on the field who had experienced less than optimal teams. They related that in some cases a poorly run team is worse than no team at all. Former team members also expressed the wish to be better trained before they went and the need for better tools to help them process the experience once home.

The result of those conversations is this book. We write it for those church leaders, missionaries, and team leaders who need information to make their short-term mission team a positive and fruitful experience for everyone involved.

## VWAP DEFINED

Just what is a VWAP? How is it different from any other vacation? What distinguishes it from any number of Christian tour groups? Let's start with a definition.

---

A Vacation with a Purpose is a short-term trip involving a group of people seeking the opportunity as a team to

- experience a different culture,
- interact personally with individuals of that culture,
- serve the nationals and/or Christian workers in the culture, and
- become "world Christians" through personal and spiritual growth derived from the experience.

---

The statement above provides a good working definition for Vacation with a Purpose, but let's make certain that we share the same terminology.

### Short-Term
For the purposes of this book, *short-term* means one to two weeks in length. (We write this at the risk of offending those who have given their entire lives to missionary service and consider anything less than five years "short-term," and anything less than two years, unthinkable!) Today, travel is such that a team can arrive at a destination in only one day, whereas in the past the trip may have taken several weeks! Thus, shorter trips with a considerable amount of time in the host community are more feasible.

In our experience, many of those attracted to short-term missions are single and/or young adults with limited vacation time or a hesitancy about using their entire vacation for this purpose. A project of under two weeks is of great interest and entirely feasible for this particular group. Teams comprising college students or retired adults could very well be longer in duration.

The following are examples of VWAPs of various durations:

*Nine Days:* Leave on Saturday and return the following Sunday. This trip appeals to people who only want or are able to miss one week of work. Some people prefer a trip that ends on Saturday so they have a day to unpack and rest before returning to work.

*Twelve Days:* Some teams that travel from west to east like to schedule trips that leave Thursday after work and return Monday evening, a week and a half later. Thus, team members miss just one full week of work, and an additional day of the two adjacent weeks.

*Fifteen Days:* This trip involves two weeks away from work and is attractive to those who have more vacation flexibility. It also allows for travel to a farther destination and more time in the host country.

## Team
A Vacation with a Purpose is more than a group of individuals who spend time traveling on the same bus and eating at the same restaurants. Team building, team growth, and teamwork are integral components of the VWAP experience.

## Experience a Different Culture
Due to increased media coverage, people today are able to catch glimpses of, and experience secondhand, various cultures around the world. A second-hand experience is not as compelling as a hands-on interaction with a culture, however. So a great many of today's adults are seizing opportunities to personally encounter the people of the cultures they have seen.

A different culture is not necessarily a non-North American one. Some cultures throughout the United States and Canada may be worlds apart from your own: inner-city poor, native Americans, and ethnic groups are a few examples.

## Interact Personally
To have meaningful opportunities to work alongside members of the host community, worshiping, working, and living together.

## To Serve
To make a significant and encouraging contribution, *as defined by the host group.*

## World Christians
Followers of Jesus Christ with an increasing awareness of their membership in, and responsibility to, the global community. These are people whose commitment to the spiritual, physical, and emotional health of their world neighbors stems from their own relationship with Jesus Christ.

## A POP QUIZ: HOW WELL DO YOU KNOW WHAT A VWAP IS?

Determine which of the following four sample trips corresponds to the VWAP definition.

❏ *Example One:* This is a trip to a small village in the Dominican Republic. The team works with the local church to construct additional classrooms in a church-based school. They sleep on the floor of the church. They participate in worship services and spend several afternoons playing with children. Team members have the opportunity to spend a night in the homes of church members. The last two days are spent at the beach and touring.

❏ *Example Two:* The team goes to a large U.S. city and stays at a local hotel. The afternoons are spent presenting a vacation Bible school to inner-city children; mornings are spent in preparation. A part of each evening is spent in discussions, with representatives from agencies and churches working in the inner-city network. Community-based ministries come and present the needs of people living in the inner city and programs designed to address the needs.

❏ *Example Three:* On this trip, sixteen people are sent to a large city in Asia. In groups of two or three, they are sent out each day by their host to work at various church-sponsored social service agencies in that city. After work they go alone or in pairs to the homes of local church members where they have dinner and sleep. During the final two days, the entire group meets at a retreat center to share experiences and work through group debriefing exercises.

❏ *Example Four:* This is a five-day trip to Mexico City. Two days are for travel. Team members spend one day being shown a local development project in a poor community. The next two days are spent sightseeing, with an emphasis on education and exposure to the Mexican culture. The team stays in the dorms of a Christian boarding school that is not in session.

### How Did You Do? Evaluating the Examples

Do these examples fit our working definition of a Vacation with a Purpose? Example One clearly does: The team *experiences a new culture,* and they *meaningfully interact* with and *serve* its members by playing with children, working alongside the adults, and worshiping with the church community.

Example Two is less clearly defined. The team is *experiencing a different culture* (providing the team members themselves are not from the inner city) and they are *interacting* with children and adults who are intimately involved with the inner city. But is the service criterion being met? *Remember that the significance of the service is defined by the host group.* In this example ask if the host feels that leaving the community at night is a problem. If so, it may mitigate against effective service.

Example Three is an excellent model for summer deputation programs.

You may have had your first exposure to the mission field in this type of setting. However, this example lacks the teamwork nature of the Vacations with a Purpose model. The team element greatly enhances the benefits of VWAP. Through the constant proximity to each other, team members learn from, lean on, encourage, and help one another. For many, this may be their first experience in real community. Furthermore, this community experience is of great interest to the host community.

Example Four is certainly a valid option. However, it does not qualify as a VWAP project. While taken for the purpose of education and exposure, the trip has limited interaction and service. Such a trip can be worthwhile, but the material in this book may not relate to the issues involved in this type of travel experience.

It is important to realize that neither the definition on page 18 nor the contents of this book are the only way to do a VWAP. We hope our working definition will allow you to determine the design of your trip as well as offer a basis for evaluating the trip and its results.

## A WORD ABOUT THE FORMAT

This book is designed to be a step-by-step handbook for team leaders and includes pages for recording everything from logistics to insights, tear-out forms that can be photocopied for your VWAP team members, a checklist to monitor your progress, and a fourteen-day journal for team leaders to record their reflections during the trip. This manual will become a permanent record and souvenir of your particular trip.

This book is designed to be used with the companion team member's manual. We suggest that you review the contents of that manual; become familiar with what team members will face in this process. In this leader's volume there are references referring to the pages in the team member's manual where matching material is found. However, their manual does not contain all the information in this volume.

Before you rush ahead, you need some folks to work with. A VWAP is not a solo operation. Planning it should *not* be the responsibility of just one person from your church. Develop a team of interested individuals to serve as a planning committee for the trip. It is helpful if one person from that planning committee (preferably from the church staff) serves as the team leader's staff liaison. Throughout the book, we will refer to the tasks of all three: team leader(s), planning committee, and staff liaison.

# CHAPTER TWO

# BENEFITS TO TEAM MEMBERS

**"**Jill took a deep breath of the salty sea air and soaked in the sights of the dusty mission station where she had just arrived with her twenty teammates. A young orphan's tiny hand in hers felt somehow comforting and familiar in this strange place. Over the laughter of children, she heard the groans of passing school buses on their way to disgorge tired field-workers in the tin and cardboard shantytown that was their home. After months of work as part of the Vacations with a Purpose (VWAP) leadership team, Jill was finally seeing the orphanage and meeting the people she had been praying for. Like the others on her team, Jill had practiced her Spanish, prepared songs, games, and lessons for the vacation Bible school, and prepared her heart to help the missionaries in whatever way she could.

As the days passed, the long hours she spent clearing rocks and brush where a church foundation would be poured seemed fulfilling, not as tedious as she had imagined. She was somehow uplifted by the hard work, especially when she and her teammates would sing old spirituals, much to the delight of the nationals working with them.

But it was the evenings that meant the most to her. After a hard day of labor, she enjoyed the chance to gather with her team and talk about the day. During those talks, everything she had been seeing and feeling seemed to come together. She thought about the few hours of gracious hospitality shown by the shantytown family she had visited, how they had offered her an upended crate for a stool and a few berries spirited home from the fields as a meal. She listened as a team member cried in confusion and sadness that so many godly people were living in such squalor, while the food they were harvesting was destined for the tables of those who had never known hunger.

Jill nodded in agreement as another teammate shared how he had been touched by the Sunday service. Everyone, it seemed, had been there: his coworkers, the immaculately groomed town doctor, the dirty and sickly village children and their weary parents, and the missionaries. They all raised their arms and voices in praise to the God of them all.

For a few days after returning home, she enjoyed recounting tales of her two-week Vacation with a Purpose. But with each passing day her little stories rang hollow to her, when she realized that her listeners couldn't really understand the meaning behind them. Then she noticed that the comforts and familiar sights and sounds at home seemed less comforting, less familiar. No longer content to amble by the homeless man who begged for coins near her apartment, she now wanted to know his name, to listen to his story, his hopes, his pains. Racial slurs and jokes about "lazy foreigners" had always made her feel uncomfortable; now they made her angry.

A short time later, Jill realized that she could no longer be content in her cozy, familiar world. She resolved to be an agent of compassion and of change. In whatever small way she could, she would help others to see people as God sees them: each one with a name, a face, a story; each one created in the image of God and for whom Christ died on the cross. **"**

❖ ❖ ❖

What happens in the lives of the team members who participate in Vacations with a Purpose? What is the value of investing precious time and money in such short-term ventures? Isn't it better to just send the money spent on a VWAP to the particular mission site so they can use it as they choose? Wouldn't that be a wiser and more practical use of funds? These are the types of questions leaders are asked again and again.

Such questions do not recognize the potential impact a trip can make on a participant such as Jill. At times a sending church can become so "project" oriented that they lose sight of the potential for growth and maturity among the team members. Jill and others who give their vacations to serve brothers and sisters abroad can be shaken to the core. Their approach to the world can become less like "Sixty Minutes" and more like the unchanging and compassionate heart of Christ.

Two weeks changed Jill's life. On a VWAP the Holy Spirit seems to have access to our lives in a fresh way. The possibilities for growth are as numerous and many-faceted as the participants. Therefore, don't expect everyone to benefit in the same way. One missions pastor explained to me that they wanted only those seriously considering full-time missionary service to go on teams; consequently this became a criteria in their interviewing process. They were limiting what God could do by their one-dimensional orientation. St. Paul was certainly not looking for a full-time career in missions when he was called. The trip helps individuals and congregations further develop and experience the challenges and sacrifices that accompany Jesus' call to follow Him.

Pastor and author Bruce Larson has said that when God wants to teach us something He takes us on a trip. Travel seems to be one of God's favorite primers for teaching us about Himself. In confronting the unfamiliar we learn to see things as they really are. Remember how John Bunyan's Pilgrim learned about the Truth in his journey away from the comforts of home? Or recall how the patriarch Joseph was plucked as a boy from his family and sent on a journey to Egypt where he learned about God's miraculous providence. In Mark Twain's classic *The Prince and the Pauper* Prince Edward learns many of life's important lessons during his days as a commoner. God has specific things to teach each person on a VWAP trip. But one thing is certain: *God wants to teach all of us the mind and character of Jesus Christ* (Philippians 2:5). VWAPs exist to make us more like Jesus.

To better comprehend this Christlikeness let's take a look at two Scripture passages. In Luke 7:12-14, we read, "As he approached the town gate, a dead person was being carried out—the only son of his mother, and she was a widow. When the Lord saw her, *his heart went out to her* and he said, 'Don't cry.' Then he went up and touched the coffin and those carrying it stood still. He said, 'Young man, I say to you get up!' The dead man sat up and began to talk, and Jesus gave him back to his mother." And in Matthew 14:14, we read, "When Jesus landed and saw a large crowd, *he had compassion on them* and healed their sick" (emphasis added).

In both incidents Jesus' interaction is marked by compassion. At least four distinct elements comprise His compassion, taking it far beyond simple pity or sympathy.

## SEEING

This seems elementary, but the Scriptures point out again and again that Jesus was actively watching what went on around Him. In the midst of the normal coming and going around the town gate he "saw" a particular woman and her pain. He "saw" something more than a mass of humanity in the large crowd. Jesus looked at the world around Him and saw what others did not see.

Traveling to an unfamiliar place can open the eyes of a VWAP participant. Remember how Jill "soaked in the sights"? She began to see things she had only heard about. The needs in the host community opened her eyes, but as we learn in the story she continued "seeing" once she was back in her own environment. The familiar things Jill had failed to see and register before her trip could not now be ignored. Exposure had removed her blindness.

Liz is another example of a team member confronted by the dramatic contrast between wealth and poverty she saw as she walked wide-eyed through the streets of Haiti. During the second team meeting she blurted out the question that had been taking shape in her mind: "How can some people live so comfortably when poverty sits on the street in front of their gate?" The leader turned the tables and asked if there weren't sections in their own towns where this kind of disparity existed. Furthermore, were they guilty of the same blindness, ignoring people in their own church communities with needs they couldn't or wouldn't see?

Participants in a cross-cultural setting often begin to see as Jesus saw. When they return home scales seem to fall from their eyes and they are given new sight. They see what they did not see before.

## UNDERSTANDING

During Jesus' time on earth funerals and widowhood were nothing out of the ordinary. Yet Jesus "saw" behind the usual ordinary events to the individual. Jesus saw and understood the pain and sorrow of this one widow. He empathized with her loss. Similarly, in the Matthew account, Jesus sees more than a crowd. He understands that they are hungry for meaning, and thirsty for truth.

During Jill's time at the orphanage she began to move from "seeing" into "understanding." Interacting with the people, she saw obvious needs and an education began to take place. The children Jill visited in the orphanage were often abandoned by parents who were too poor to care for them. Others were left on the streets by parents who battle with alcohol or drugs. It only takes eyes to see a child who needs to be loved, fed, clothed, and educated; it takes something more to understand why. Jill's education was going far beyond books, stories, and the evening news.

Often we react to people's needs rather than trying to understand the complex issues at work in their lives. We fail to see that understanding is the foundation upon which other responses may be placed. True understanding requires that we educate ourselves to the social, political, and spiritual implications of what we see.

It was toward the end of another trip that Marilu's education really began. She had ample opportunity to see needs during the project, but it was the opportunity to spend the night at one of the church members' homes that pushed her past surface reactions. Marilu approached the evening hesitantly and ambivalently because of the language barriers, but together she and a fellow team member accompanied a woman home. Her overnight stay enabled her to see the hurts and hopes that lay in the midst of the poverty. She began to understand.

## FEELING

Jesus saw the widow and "his heart went out to her." He did more than see and understand a woman bereaved of her husband and son. She was more than a statistic. Jesus felt her anguish and became emotionally involved.

In Jill's account one is able to sense that she became emotionally involved in the lives of the people in the orphanage and the community surrounding it. As she saw and understood the people she allowed God to draw her in emotionally. This "drawing in" can be frightening because it makes us vulnerable.

The children's hospital in Port-au-Prince, Haiti, began to produce this sort of vulnerability in another team member named David. The team constructed gingerbread playhouses, giving them plenty of opportunities to playfully interact with the children. During one team meeting David shared a profound realization. That morning as he held a child in his arms he remembered the countless times he had watched TV footage of needy children around the world. Overwhelmed with conviction, he recalled that in his discomfort he simply switched the channel. But now, the children were all too real. It was as if God were saying to him, "So how are you going to switch the channel now?" He realized he had allowed himself to "feel" and would need to respond to the multitude of needs existing in his world rather than change the channel.

In a short two-week vacation team members can come face to face with the needs, sorrows, and joys of brothers and sisters of another culture. When intellectual knowledge becomes heartfelt understanding, the head and heart work in tandem and the compassion of Christ is seen. Just as Jesus' "heart went out" to the grieving woman, God breaks our hearts, freeing us to feel deeply. Working side by side with one another we are invited into a vibrant encounter with new friends, our God, and ourselves.

## RESPONDING

After seeing, understanding, and feeling, Jesus' work still was not done. There was something else He had to *do*. He raised the son of the grieving widow; He healed and then fed the broken and hungry crowd. Jesus' life on earth was marked by a response to the needs of those He saw around Him. Our hope for all participants in Vacations with a Purpose is their growth in desire and willingness to respond—to do something.

Responding is the culmination to Jill's seeing the orphans, understanding their plight, and becoming emotionally involved. Her response began on the trip, but when she gets home she is "no longer content to amble by the homeless man who begged for coins near her apartment." The character of Christ is filtering into the world all around her.

Responding does not simply benefit the outside world. It may also represent a willingness to let God into our own lives. Allowing God to enter in opens the heart and mind to a good many things we may be avoiding. Jeff went on a team to make a difference in the lives of the Dominican people. He worked hard to construct the building the people needed. Yet eight days of working and living with team members and his hosts taught him that the most significant thing he encountered was his *own* selfishness. God utilized the circumstances, the people, and the building project to unmask what was easily avoided and rationalized at home. He had a heart like the Grinch's. It was ten sizes too small! Now what was he going to do about it?

As we mentioned, the changes that occur in the lives of team members through VWAP's lessons in compassion are as numerous as the number of individuals that go. But several responses seem to prevail in most team members. Our experience, as well as the research conducted by Jones and Engel, shows that short-term mission participants are more likely than other church members to

- donate time and financial resources to missions;
- become actively involved in church leadership as elders, deacons,

Sunday school teachers, etc.;
- become more involved in local community outreach;
- become more involved in the local church and its ministry;
- consider becoming a long-term missionary either now or in the future; and
- consider evangelism a higher priority in their own lives.[1]

A Vacation with a Purpose is eye-opening, heartbreaking, and mind-boggling. God takes us on a journey and then calls us to respond to Him. Certainly God can teach us to see, to understand, to feel, and to respond without our ever leaving home. But the experience, profound and personal in its confrontation of need, may be just what our hearts need to learn the compassion of Christ.

---

NOTE    1. James Engel and Jerry D. Jones, *Baby Boomers and the Future of World Missions* (Orange, CA: Management Development Associates, 1989), page 39.

# CHAPTER THREE

# BENEFITS TO
# THE SENDING CHURCH

*Question: If twenty people from your church get on an airplane and head off for a Vacation with a Purpose, how many people are on the team?*
*Answer: The whole church!*

One of the exciting benefits of Vacations with a Purpose is the impact the team has on the local church or ministry. For each team member, dozens of others can and should be involved. The much-needed prayer and the emotional and financial demands require the support of a larger body. As the larger group invests itself in the experience, the enthusiasm and concern for the project reverberates throughout the congregation. Team members become ambassadors of the larger group.

When team members return, their renewed passion and vision can be a spark igniting the ministry of the entire church. Let's look at some ways churches are impacted by returning teams.

## Outreach

Local ministries have a tendency at times to be inwardly focused. As we attempt to meet the needs of those in the pews, we may lose sight of the needs that exist outside the church. Once a team from your church has the opportunity to touch lives outside the group, their enthusiasm can be contagious. As congregations cultivate an outward focus, doors of awareness swing open. Missionaries, internationals, and "outsiders" to the community begin to feel there is a place of understanding for them in the church.

## Renewal

There's something powerful in the way a team is affected by the chance to worship with Christians in a different cultural context. Perhaps it's due to the deep sense of kinship felt between newly acquainted brothers and sisters in Christ. It may be because they are jolted out of old, familiar styles of worship. Perhaps it's because a cultural cocoon breaks open revealing to the team members that God has been quietly transforming them.

Whatever renewal the team members experience seems to make its way back home with them. The impact made on the team through the lives of the missionaries and host church members is like a healing balm that can spread rapidly, warming your whole church.

## Community

The team members' experience in the field is marked by a daily need to rely on others. Often in our own communities we are not forced to work, serve, or socialize with people who are different from us. However, team participants do not have the option of choosing whom they will travel and work with. They are placed in a situation where, often for the first time in their lives, they experience the fullness of the imagery of the different parts of the body working together in community (1 Corinthians 12:12-36). Community living can be the catalyst by which people learn to appreciate those they never had the time or inclination to notice before. It also affords an arena in which conflict resolution and forgiveness are seen as natural parts of Christian living. A team that has experienced the joys (and perturbations) of community living will bring home a model that affects the whole congregation/ministry.

## Leadership Development

Traveling with a group of relative strangers, experiencing the awkwardness of the cross-cultural setting, seeing the Christian life expressed by others from a different background, surviving the discomforts of spartan living conditions—these all provide a unique forum for recognizing leadership traits in others. By delegating responsibility for one facet of the trip to each team member, you provide opportunities for leadership to develop and grow. One singles leader in a large urban church says that 50 percent of his lay leaders over a four-year period had come from VWAP teams. He adds that several team members have also gone into positions of leadership as elders, deacons, and Christian education leaders. The leadership development potential is a great boost, not only to the singles and young adults in the church, but to the entire congregation as well.

❖  ❖  ❖

A Vacation with a Purpose develops the *faith*, the *focus*, the *relationships*, and the *leadership* of the entire congregation.

CHAPTER FOUR

# BENEFITS TO
# THE HOST MISSIONARY

**"**Charlie flipped through the three envelopes that had arrived for him with the last shipment of supplies from the home office. There was the usual letter from his mother, who never seemed to forget to write; a letter from a Bible study group from his home church; and one from Bill Jenkins.

Charlie and Bill had hit it off the first day Bill arrived at the San Pablo water project with a team of the sorriest looking volunteers Charlie thought he had ever seen. He was a little embarrassed as he recalled his initial thoughts.

"This must be the work team they said was coming. A bunch of office workers who spent a fortune getting here to see a 'genuine' missionary and real live 'natives,'" he had said to himself. "I'll probably lose ten good days of work translating while they're here, and another ten after they've gone around apologizing to the people of San Pablo for their offensive behavior."

What a delight to find out how wrong his first impression had been. Bill had later explained that the team had spent several weeks practicing the language and learning about the Latin American church. They had even had a class session with a former missionary to the area who had explained local customs and value systems.

He smiled to himself and, with a silent apology to his mom, opened Bill's letter first.

Dear Charlie and Pat,

Please accept this check for the purchase of the irrigation equipment you've been hoping to buy. After working with you for those ten short days last year, the team and I couldn't get your big plans out of our minds. Steve is the one who came up with the idea of telling everyone we could think of about your project and your work with the kind people of San Pablo. We all had a great time sharing with the people at our offices about God's love while explaining what the money was being raised for. A lot of people who have never set foot in a church were happy to pitch in.

I was really glad you let the team take you and Pastor Jose to dinner the last night. We enjoyed hearing more about your lives and work, but even more, we enjoyed just talking and laughing. I really felt like we'd all known each other a long time. Nancy said she never knew missionaries would be so "normal"!

About eight of us from the team have continued to meet regularly to pray for you. Having been with you for those few days seems to make it much easier to pray. We have a much better idea of your work and your needs. A lot of others from our congregation have been really interested in hearing about our trip. Many of them have expressed an interest in continuing the project next spring. Please let us know if this would meet a need of yours.

Charlie had a hard time reading the last few sentences through the warm tears that were pooling at the lower edges of his eyes. Sometimes he and Pat had wondered if anyone remembered they were down here.

After a lot of prayer, and long talks with the mission pastor at our church, I have decided to put my engineering degree to work on the mission field. You two, and the other missionaries on your team, gave me a powerful insight into what hard, discouraging, lonely *joy* there is in serving Christ as a missionary. I have written to your agency with my application. My teammates and I have been praying that I might be placed with you on the water project.

> Your brother in Christ,
> Bill **"**

❖  ❖  ❖

Are Vacations with a Purpose a blessing or a curse to missionaries? For many, unfortunately, it has been the latter. Some mission agencies have, with very good reason, been hesitant to plunge into the tricky waters of short-term teams. They've heard the stories: poorly trained teams doing more harm than good; poor communication between the team and the agency; the nightmarish logistical burdens imposed on missionaries; and the inadequate team leadership.

But an increasing number are like Charlie. More and more mission agencies are finding that a properly trained, adequately supervised team with an attitude of meekness and service can be an unexpected blessing. Charlie's story is actually compiled from conversations we have had with several missionaries. Many of them are contacting their mission boards with reports of their positive experiences with short-term teams. Below are some of the benefits they've told us about.

### Exposure to Their Work

What organization or missionary would not want to expose people to a work they feel is very important? Team members on the field get firsthand exposure to the agency's day-to-day work.

## People Catch the Missionary's Vision

Missionaries have told us that one of their most difficult responsibilities is conveying their vision to real or potential supporters through media presentations and testimonies. They say it is difficult to communicate the real essence of their ministry. Photographs and stories about people don't convey the nuances of the lives that are being touched. But what a joy to have people come and see for themselves! No amount of videotapes and prayer letters can say as much as a week spent living, walking, and talking with the missionary on the field.

## Missionaries Are Encouraged and Affirmed

Life in a foreign culture can be frustrating, lonely, and discouraging. Having people come and support their work can be a tremendous boost to the missionary—emotionally, physically, and spiritually. Knowing that team members will continue praying after they return home can make the miles seem shorter and the work less lonely.

## Long-Term Relationships

A VWAP team that becomes involved with a missionary creates a connection that can last far beyond the one or two weeks the team is on the field. We've seen many churches establish long-term partnerships with missionaries and/or mission projects. To the missionary, these partnerships mean constant prayer support, additional workers, financial support, and a sense that there are people out there who won't let the missionary be forgotten.

## Future Missions Workers

Researchers Jerry D. Jones and James F. Engel published a study, *Baby Boomers and the Future of World Missions*, investigating how to involve the generation known as "baby boomers" in world missions. (Baby boomers, Americans born between 1946 and 1964, constitute the largest single demographic subgroup in the current U.S. population.) Their survey revealed that 54 percent of this group are open to considering career missionary service. However, that statistic jumps to 74 percent among those who have participated in a short-term mission experience. Fully 80 percent of this latter group claim an interest in missionary service upon retirement.[1]

## Financial Support

Jones and Engel's research also shows a link between short-term mission involvement and increased mission giving. They conclude that there "are clear indications that prior short-term service on the field sharply increases [the baby boomer's] interest in both financial giving and in a missionary career. Given their high overall reluctance to each of these areas, we are forced to conclude that a short-term missionary service program is a must."[2]

They also report that today's young adults are more likely to donate money directly to a work or individual with which they are personally acquainted, rather than to organizations. Missionaries on the field, like

Charlie in our story, have seen this type of giving in action. Funds that were not available in their budgets are provided by teams who wish to contribute directly to the people they have come to love.

NOTES    1. James Engel and Jerry D. Jones, *Baby Boomers and the Future of World Missions* (Orange, CA: Management Development Associates, 1989), page 32.
        2. Engel and Jones, page 28.

# CHAPTER FIVE

# BENEFITS TO THE HOST COMMUNITY/CHURCH

66Pastor Manuel looked over the Americans as Mitch, his missionary friend, introduced the team to the congregation. Smiling as convincingly as he could, Pastor Manuel tried to hide his disappointment.

With a few others from his small congregation, Pastor Manuel had been praying that the simple but lovely church building they had been slowly erecting would be finished within a year. Then one day, Mitch had asked him if he would consider allowing a team from the United States to come and assist his parishioners. Manuel had been overjoyed. The congregation was so weary of working evenings and weekends. And now, only a handful of men ever came to help.

But as Pastor Manuel surveyed the motley group, he wondered if they would be any help at all. For starters, there were only nine of them, not the fifteen to twenty he had hoped to see. Worse, in his opinion, was the fact that only three were men. And he confessed to thinking that two of the six women looked too old to be capable of much work at all.

He watched the congregation's teenagers finish the welcome drama they had prepared for the American guests. Pushing down his doubts he began to mentally assign team members to the three families who had offered to host them. Just then, Señora de Fuente appeared at his side.

"Pastor," she whispered, "would you mind letting me take one of these Norteamericanos home to my house? I know I wasn't willing earlier, but now that I see them, I think it might not be so difficult." Before he could answer, another couple from the congregation echoed her request. Soon his list of three host families had grown to seven.

Throughout the week, the host families kept Pastor Manuel entertained with stories of their guests. They laughed as they tried to pronounce the difficult names. They proudly reported their progress in teaching the Spanish language to their charges.

By the third day, Pastor Manuel realized he might have been a little too quick to judge this group of laborers. He'd been told by Don Pepe, the foreman, that although the team didn't know much about laying block, they were quick learners and willing to work very hard. "And," Don Pepe marveled, "you should see how the women work!"

To satisfy his curiosity, Pastor Manuel and his wife, Laura, went to the work site the following afternoon. They tried not to gawk as they watched the women in big, muddy boots and oversized work gloves mixing cement, pushing wheelbarrows of mortar, and carrying block and rebar. Laura noticed, with a soft chuckle, that this busy little bunch had attracted quite a crowd of onlookers from the surrounding neighborhood.

That night at the evening service Laura could not concentrate on the songs she was leading. Thoughts of everything she had seen that day kept making her lose her place in the chorus. Finally, she spoke up.

"Brothers and sisters," she said to the sixty or so adults, teens, and children in front of her, "I feel I must say something to you. I was at the work site today and saw our visitors working with Don Pepe and his two helpers. When I saw how willing they were to work hard, especially the 'old ladies'"—she winked at the two senior team members, who beamed at the compliment—"I scolded myself for not being there at their side. Tomorrow I'm going to put on my old clothes and be there with them at 7:30 a.m. I challenge all of you, especially the women, to do the same!"

What a crew assembled the next morning! Men and women from throughout the congregation had accepted the challenge and were eagerly joining the effort. Antonio and his whole family were there, all dressed in identical khaki work clothes. Maria, a wrinkled eighty-six-year-old woman, insisted on doing her share, boasting, "I'm as strong as any teenager!" She left no doubters as she hauled heavy buckets of mortar in each hand. Although the strength ebbed from her arms during the course of the day, the wide smile never left her wrinkled face.

On the final day, at a gala but bittersweet farewell fiesta, Pastor Manuel pulled the team leader aside.

"You've finished one entire wall of our building and for that I'm very grateful. Perhaps we'll finish this building more quickly because of your help. In any case, you've done something more, something that cannot be measured. You've shared our lives, our homes, and our meals with us. You've given love and encouragement to our little congregation with your presence here. We will always remember you and thank God for you."

❖ ❖ ❖

Any Vacation with a Purpose team has a great opportunity to have a significant impact upon their host church. Team members may not realize the effects that simply living with people can have. What we receive from our hosts is so much more obvious. The nationals give from their want and we from our surplus. Nonetheless, the team can make a lasting impact in several areas.

## RELATIONSHIPS

Members of churches in other countries appreciate the relationships they form with team members. They are excited about the possibilities of developing friendships with North American Christians who will pray for and with them in their work and ministry. Team members will find that the most-requested souvenir is their address.

Sadly, developing lasting friendships often seems to be more important to the host group than to the team members. So often, North Americans focus on the project and evaluate the success of the trip by what they get done. The truth is, our hosts sometimes prefer to talk with team members in their living rooms rather than lay block with them on the construction site!

## CULTURE

We need to remember that the team members are not the only ones who have a cross-cultural experience! The host group is often amused by the behavior of their visitors, especially the participation of women in traditionally male tasks. And since U.S. and Canadian citizens come from many races and cultures, the nationals are exposed to a broad spectrum of the Body of Christ.

On one VWAP, the children's favorite team member was an Asian-American. The team later realized that the children assumed from looking at him that he must know kung fu. The only Asians they had ever seen were in television martial arts films. Children followed Tim wherever he went, attempting to imitate the martial arts moves they had seen in the movies. There was nothing Tim could say to convince them that he was as American as any of his teammates and that he knew no more kung fu than they did!

Another team took a VWAP to both Haiti and the Dominican Republic. Arriving in the Dominican Republic, they brought with them stories of their Haitian experience. These were often of more interest to the Dominicans than stories of the U.S. culture. The Dominicans were fascinated to hear Haitian songs and the descriptions of their next door neighbors. Haiti and the Dominican Republic share the same island home, but their languages and culture are varied and distinctive. The team became a bridge builder between the two countries.

## AFFIRMATION

National church members have told us they are often renewed and rejuvenated by the simple presence of North Americans who come as servants. Rightly or wrongly, they perceive us as rich and powerful, and they are touched when we come in genuine humility.

A nurse and her husband in the Caribbean formed a long-lasting relationship with a singles team from Florida. Members of the team have continued to affirm this couple and their work through letters, visits, and medical supplies.

In the five years since they worked together, this couple has expressed time and again how much love and affirmation they felt from that team.

Over the years, when members of that team have gotten married, a beautifully wrapped wedding present appears from a grateful and gracious couple in the Caribbean.

## FINANCIAL

Very often the team is the vehicle God uses to answer the prayers of an individual congregation. One singles ministry sent two members to scout projects in a Latin American country. In talking with the representatives of a mission agency at work in that country, they learned that a congregation in a remote, rural village was praying for the means to build a Christian school for the villagers. The mission agency confessed that they were aware of the need but lacked the funds or staff to assist with the project. The two felt compelled to make the three-hour drive to meet the villagers.

They met with the pastor and explained that they wanted to take a team someplace where they could live and work alongside Christians from another culture. They asked if the school planners would allow them to become involved in the school project. They related that team members were willing to provide the funds, as well as help build the school.

The planners were elated but cautious. After the building was completed, the hosts confessed to having doubted that the funds they had prayed for so long were finally going to be provided. They were like those Jerusalem Christians who fervently prayed for Peter's release from jail, and then refused to believe he was standing at the door. God had answered their prayers in a way that totally confounded their expectations.

# PART TWO
# GETTING STARTED

*In part 1 we described how a Vacation with a Purpose can benefit the team members, the churches they represent, and the host community to which they minister.*

*In part 2 you will find the tools to begin planning a VWAP for your own church or group. Before you start making your plans, however, you need to ask yourself some important questions.*

*Discuss the questions on the following pages and fill in your answers in the spaces provided. Think carefully about your responses. They will set the agenda for your vacation, helping to determine where you go, who you work with, and who you contact during the preparation process. They also provide a necessary point of reference for choosing the type of VWAP you design for your group. After your first trip is completed, refer back to these questions for help in planning a strategy for future teams.*

## IMPORTANT "GETTING STARTED" QUESTIONS

1. What are your dreams (not only for this year, but down the road)? What do you want to accomplish?

   a. In the area of leadership development:

   b. In terms of a specific project goal:

   c. In terms of contact with/support for missionaries:

   d. In terms of team dynamics and/or personal growth of your team members:

   e. In terms of exposure to/relationships with nationals:

2. Should you plan the logistics yourselves, or seek the assistance of an agency? Your answer will be based on the resources available to your church or group.

  a. List the people who can put you in touch with foreign nationals or mission agencies.

  b. List those in your group who speak a foreign language.

  c. List those who have traveled extensively for work, school, or business.

  d. Who might have the time to do much of the pre-trip on-field logistics?

  e. List others who, because of their specific area of expertise, might be considered as resources or contacts for a particular culture.

With these answers in mind, you are ready to begin selecting the person or persons who will lead the VWAP team.

# CHAPTER SIX

# CHOOSING THE TEAM LEADER

The person who leads the team sets the tone for the type of experience each team member will have. If the team leader is calm in the face of unexpected events, the team will respond with a similar attitude. If the leader exhibits emotional and spiritual maturity, he or she will likely elicit the same from the team members. If the leader is irresponsible, complains, and gossips, the post-trip evaluations will likely reflect the negativity of the leader and diminish the quality of the experience.

## QUALIFICATIONS FOR TEAM LEADERSHIP

How does the planning committee choose the team leader? What are the important criteria to consider? By the time you reach this chapter of the book, you may already have chosen a leader. If not, add these four essentials to your list of selection criteria:

1. *The team leader should have some familiarity with the culture and language of the area to be visited.* This may very well be impossible if no one from your church has ever traveled in the area. However, at the very least, the team leader should be experienced in foreign travel, preferably Third-World travel. If the team leader does not speak the local language, take someone who does. It can make things much easier as well as sparing the hosts the burden of translation.

2. *The team leader should have a reputation for spiritual maturity.* Does he or she have the maturity in Christ to help other team members glean the varied and sometimes difficult spiritual applications of the Vacation with a Purpose? For example, some team members may be unaccustomed to different forms of worship and may become confused or even frightened by what they see. A leader with maturity can help team members process the different things they are seeing and experiencing.

3. *The team leader should have a reputation for personal maturity.* Has this person handled difficulty in his or her personal life? Is he or she known to treat people fairly, sensitively, and responsibly? Will he or she be strong enough to shoulder the minor and not-so-minor crises that

may arise? Will he or she lead capably without being autocratic?

4. *The team leader should have a reputation for being good-natured.* Would people describe this person as congenial, patient, relaxed, flexible, and possessing a good sense of humor? Situations can become stressful on a VWAP, so it is crucial that the leader be able to "roll with the punches." A rigid person serving as leader may alienate many of the team members and/or hosts and thus work against the overall objectives of the trip.

It goes without saying that the team leader need not be a pastor. Many lay members of your congregation or group are qualified to be effective leaders. However, team leaders will benefit greatly from the guidance and encouragement of the pastoral staff.

## ONE LEADER OR TWO?

This book is written from the perspective that each team will have one identifiable leader. Our experience has shown us that this works best. Usually the team leader ends up choosing one or more team members as advisors or prayer partners who can be counted on for support and assistance. Nevertheless, some groups may prefer sending a team of leaders. When this is the case, keep the following in mind:

1. *Each identified leader should have a clearly defined role.* One may be responsible for all of the logistical aspects of the trip, coordinating the details and working with the hosts, while another handles the spiritual side, coordinating the team's devotional times and the presentations in churches. One may be the team's primary liaison with the foreign nationals, while the other interacts mainly with the team members. Kim has twice led teams on which her husband was a team member. The Latin American hosts often addressed their comments and questions to her husband, whom they felt more comfortable perceiving as the leader.

2. *The team members should thoroughly understand the division of roles.*

3. *The team leaders should demonstrate servanthood and humility in their interactions with one another.*

4. *One of the leaders should have the final responsibility.* This is essential to avoid confusion and mistakes during emergency situations.

## THE TEAM LEADER'S JOB DESCRIPTION

A team leader needs a job description. Realistically though, if you were to hand this book to prospective leaders and ask them to consider the job, you might never get any takers! Like the proverbial journey of a thousand miles, team leadership needs to be approached one step at a time. The following job description is a first step for those considering leading a VWAP team.

## Objective

To effectively organize, prepare, and lead team members on a Vacation with a Purpose. The leader is responsible for the overall team experience while in the country and will serve as a liaison between team members and the missionaries and/or nationals with whom the team is working.

## Responsibilities

The planning committee entrusts the leader with the control and direction of the team, depending on him or her to fulfill each of the following responsibilities:

1. *Lead as a servant.* It is the leader's primary responsibility to do all he or she can to ensure that each member has a positive experience while serving on the team.
2. *Lead by delegation.* The emotional and physical demands of taking a group on a VWAP can be a tremendous responsibility for a leader to bear alone. Therefore, the leader must be committed to delegating tasks and authority to team members. A single-handed leadership style robs others of the rewards of shouldering team responsibility. (Note: While many of the following steps can be delegated, you will have the ultimate responsibility for seeing that each step is followed properly.)
3. *Plan an itinerary for the team.* The leader should work with the contacts and/or staff of the sending church as well as the host community.
4. *Schedule, organize, and hold team preparation meetings.* We suggest that prior to leaving, each team should have four to six required meetings aimed at orienting and preparing the team for the project.
5. *Encourage team member preparation spiritually, emotionally, and logistically.* Be sure each team member is informed as to the pre-departure details.
6. *Encourage team members in their fund-raising efforts.* You are not responsible for raising their money, but you need to offer suggestions on fund-raising as well as keep tabs on each member's financial progress. Collect team members' payments and deposit them in the proper account. If donations for team members come to the church office, be sure to tell them who their donors are and encourage them to write to them while on the trip.
7. *Attempt to learn as much as possible about your host country before leaving.*
8. *Follow up on any medical requirements and passport or visa requirements for each member.*
9. *If you are working with other leaders, maintain open and honest communication during the preparation time.* Once in the country, hold a brief daily meeting for all leaders. It is essential that you model teamwork for the rest of the team.
10. *Make sure all team leaders follow the rules set down by anyone in authority for the team.* These rules or guidelines may include those given by the

mission agency, the national church, or the home church.

11. *Maintain regular group devotions during the course of the trip.* Allow for informal team meetings so team members can share about the day's experiences and what God is teaching them. The team should have a devotional and/or team meeting every day.

12. *Draw out of the team members the things they are learning while on the team.* Think through the events of the day and how God may have used those experiences in people's lives.

13. *Get the team members to the destination site and home again.* This includes arranging transportation to and from your home airport.

14. *Prepare for possible emergencies.* Be aware of the medical training of people on your team. Discuss with your host the availability of medical care. Obtain emergency phone numbers for each team member. And don't forget a well-stocked first-aid kit.

15. *Handle all logistics involved in travel.* Be sure to confirm airline and ground transportation reservations, and make sure all baggage meets airline requirements and is properly identified.

16. *Be a problem solver.* When a problem seems too large to handle, don't be afraid to ask for help. Keep an accurate list of possible sources of help.

17. *Go through the debriefing material with the team while on the field.*

18. *Be debriefed after your return.* With a select group from your church/group, meet to discuss the successes and failures of the trip. Spend time reviewing the team's evaluations and the leader's insights, frustrations, and perspective. Can you identify the future leaders on your team? What experience has been gained that would be helpful to future leaders?

19. *Schedule, organize, and conduct post-trip follow-up meetings.*

20. *Pray.* Both before and during the trip.

## Challenge

The challenge for the leader can be summarized in the following exhortation: *Pray for vision!*

1. *Vision for self:* How can you grow personally during this trip?
2. *Vision for team:* What can be accomplished as a team?
3. *Vision for each team member:* What can God do in each one's life?
4. *Vision for the sending church:* How can God use this experience to enhance the life of the church and the witness of its members?

---

### LEADER'S COVENANT

I agree to lead the team going to _____

on _____, 19_____ through _____,

19_____. Relying on God, I will lead to the best of my ability and will

comply with the responsibilities outlined in the above job description.

_____

Signature                      Date

---

CHAPTER SEVEN

# CHOOSING YOUR DESTINATION

So you've decided to go on a Vacation with a Purpose. You've read the job description and chosen a leader. Confidence and support for the project have grown as you considered the benefits and goals in store for your church. Now the time has come to decide where you're going.

Perhaps this decision has already been made by the encouragement and support given for a particular area. A former missionary or missions committee may have suggestions about where to go. But if you're at square one, consider the following factors as you make your decision. Use the space provided to make notes to refer to later in the process.

## QUESTIONS TO ASK YOURSELF

1. *What are our cost limitations?* Will each team member be largely responsible for his or her own costs? If so, how much can we expect each person to pay? What is the typical income of the people we are hoping to attract? Are they twenty-five-year-olds just starting their careers? Are they single parents? Are they thirty-five-year-olds with a strong, steady income and no children?

2. *Do we have a preference for a particular country or region?* Would we like to go to Mexico (or the Caribbean) because it's close? Do we want to head toward Guatemala because we have been following the prayer letters of missionaries there for years? Are we excited about a project we have supported in the past?

*49*

3. *What about language?* Do we have Spanish speakers in our group? If so, should we go to an area where Spanish is spoken? If no people in the group have foreign language skills, should we head for a mission project with a large bilingual staff? Maybe we should go to an inner-city project in the United States, a Native American village, or a country where English is spoken.

4. *What time constraints exist?* Are prospective team members limited by their jobs? (People who get only two weeks of vacation per year don't always like to use it all at once. Often, their companies won't let them.) Can we plan a longer trip and give ourselves more travel-time leeway?

5. *Do we need to consider the political situation in the country?* If the government has a history of instability, can we avoid trouble by staying out of certain cities? Has our country published a travelers' advisory for that country?

6. *How much of our time should we spend in travel?* If, for example, we would like to go to a remote mountain village, how much time will be spent simply getting there and back? If a trip is nine days long, four days traveling may be a poor use of the team's time.

7. *In choosing our destination, what resources in our own church can we tap?* Can we ask for input from the missions committee? From furloughed or returned missionaries? International students? Graduate students with experience abroad? A church member whose daughter or brother is a missionary?

8. *Should we work with a missionary agency?* Or do we feel confident working directly with the pastor in the host community?

9. *What type of accommodations are we looking for?* Will we be staying with families? In tents? Dorms? Schools? What about meal and laundry arrangements? How close is the nearest medical care? Where will the vacation portion of the trip be spent? Is there a suitable beach or resort or city nearby for rest and debriefing?

10. *Finally, do we have a particular type of project in mind?* Would we like to work on a construction site? With children? In a medical or dental clinic? Do we have professionals in our congregation whose participation we want to attract?

## VWAP DESTINATION SET-UP SHEET

Now that you have thought about the factors involved in determining a destination, begin to contact possible missionary hosts or their agencies. Contact your church mission pastor/director or the people you listed above as resources. Once you are ready to begin communicating directly with an agency or host, use this set-up sheet as a guide for collecting the necessary information.

Have it handy and refer to it whenever you discuss the proposed project by phone or in correspondence. We have often scribbled notes on several sheets of paper and have been unable to locate them quickly during a costly international call.

The questions on this sheet are meant to gather information only. It should not be used as a checklist or rating system for possible hosts. There are no right or wrong answers. Use it merely as an instrument to collect as much pertinent information as possible.

Proposed Destination

Country

City/Area

Project

Name and Phone/Address of Contact

Proposed Dates

Proposed Team Size

**Work**
1. What work is specifically needed?

2. What specific skills would be helpful?

3. What finances are needed to do the work?

4. What tools or supplies are available? What else should we try to bring?

5. Who will be overseeing the work? In the case of construction teams should we provide a contractor, or will there be one there?

6. If there is a need to hire laborers, who is responsible for their pay? How much per day for paid labor?

**Facilities**
   7. Sleeping: What are the sleeping facilities? What bedding do we need to bring?

8. Bathing: What are the facilities?

9. Power supply: Is there electricity? If not, would we have access to a generator?

10. Meeting rooms: What are the facilities for team meetings? Are the meeting rooms available at all times? Are there lights for evening meetings?

11. Cooking:

    a. What are the kitchen facilities?

    b. What are the dining facilities?

    c. What utensils are available?

d. Will the team prepare its own food?

e. Total number of breakfasts, lunches, dinners:

f. Availability of help? Cost?

g. Is local food/water available and safe? If not, what preparations do we need to make?

h. Is there refrigeration? Ice?

i. List food and beverages readily available:

j. What is the estimated cost of food per person per day? (Answer this question if you will be responsible for preparing or paying for the preparation of the team's food.)

12. Laundry: Will the team have facilities available? Would hiring nationals be appropriate?

**Transportation**

13. For the following purposes, what transportation is available on a daily basis?

    a. To and from the airport:

    b. For grocery shopping:

    c. For sightseeing:

    d. For construction materials (if team is responsible for bringing large quantities or heavy supplies):

    e. For medical emergencies:

14. What is the estimated cost of the necessary transportation?

**Service**

15. Aside from the work responsibilities, what other areas are there in which the missionaries/hosts wish to utilize the team?

16. Would they like us to participate in church services (singing, puppets, testimonies, etc.)? How many services occur during the week? How many would they like us to attend?

**Recreation**

17. What options are available for recreation (e.g., soccer or softball with host community, swimming, restaurants)?

18. What sightseeing is recommended for this team? How can team members best be exposed to this culture?

19. What destination is recommended for the rest and recreation portion of the trip? Is going there time and cost effective?

## Cultural/Religious Standards

20. Are there any cultural or religious practices team members need to be aware of?

21. a. What is the appropriate dress? Are shorts appropriate for men? For women? Are long pants permissible for women?

    b. What should not be worn?

## Emergencies

22. a. What medical facilities are available?

    b. How far is the nearest hospital, doctor, and nurse?

23. a. Can we be reached by telephone? What is the telephone number?

    b. If traveling to a remote area, will we be in radio contact with anyone?

c. Can we communicate with our home city if necessary? How?

## Local Assistance

24. Will anyone from the national church or mission agency assist us with the labor (meal preparation, laundry, on the job)?

25. Will anyone from the national church or mission agency assist us with the outreach (songs, mimes, evangelism)?

## Miscellaneous

Use this space to list questions that are particular to your group's needs.

## PLANNING THE VWAP ITINERARY

You cannot begin to plan an itinerary without talking to your host and understanding his or her expectations. Using the information you have collected on the set-up sheet, you can begin to plan a daily itinerary. The following are suggestions to keep in mind as you get started.

1. *Remember to be flexible in your planning.* Many things may change once you arrive in the country. If you are inflexible or rigid you will only be frustrated.

2. *Keep in mind the overall goals of your team when planning the team's schedule.* For example, if the team feels strongly that they are there to work on a "project," they will expect to do all they can to finish the project. If the project is not the goal, be sure to communicate that clearly prior to the trip. Remember the definition of a VWAP when doing the planning.

3. *It is your responsibility to expose the team to the particular culture and people.* If team members simply went to the site and worked without experiencing the area or its people, they would leave without a real sense of the church and country *and* their needs. Plans should enable team members to get a feel for the country they visit. This can include visits to historical sights, cathedrals, restaurants, markets, homes of the host community, church services, etc.

4. *Plan for the participants who have never been on a VWAP before.* Think from the perspective of a first-timer. Remember the first time you made a big trip? Remember the new sights and sounds, the emotional overload? Take time to recollect your initial thoughts and emotions. Things that now seem predictable, ordinary, or rather obvious to you may not seem so to the first-timers on your team! Just because you have visited certain historical sights two or three times is no reason to delete these from the itinerary. First-timers need the benefits you began with.

5. *Keep within the budget you have established.* Be flexible with your budget: various items may exceed budget; others may not. For example, you may budget to rent a van while in the country, but once there find that someone is willing to loan you theirs. Great! You came in under budget for transportation. But food prices may increase dramatically since you set the trip up. So you will spend more on food. Estimating your budget on the higher side is wise. The rule of thumb is to add about 20 percent to your estimates.

6. *It is best to have the leadership decide how to use the available time.* Working with adults naturally lends itself to group decision-making. However, allowing the team to vote on every decision may only lead to disagreements and disunity. You don't have to run the perfect democracy. Lead lovingly, but don't be afraid to use your authority and make decisions.

7. *It is not necessary to fill every second of free time.* The team members need

time to sit around talking with one another and the nationals. Often this unstructured time becomes the most significant and memorable of all.

8. *Allow time for shopping and touring.* People enjoy seeing the historical aspects of the country, such as cathedrals and museums. Many team participants intend to bring back souvenirs from the country, so be sure to schedule time for shopping.

9. *We suggest planning the vacation portion of the trip for the end of your stay.* The team will feel like they have "earned" it and will enjoy it more. This time also allows the participants to reflect on what they have learned and digest their experience.

10. *Schedule the itinerary with input from the hosts, but balance that with the needs and interests of the team.* The hosts may have many good ideas for ways your team can spend its time, but they do not understand the team as well as you do. For example, your hosts may want to schedule so many activities that the team has no time for journal writing or team devotions.

11. *Allow for some R & R time each day.* You don't need to "kill" the people physically in order for them to develop a vision for the world! Team members often complain that their busy days do not leave them enough time for journaling and time alone.

12. *Do not feel obligated to go to church services every night.* The nationals we have worked with have always understood the team's need for some time alone. It is the leader's responsibility to protect that time.

13. *Think through which touring times you will want to share with nationals.* Simply leaving the door open may create some logistical difficulties. (You may end up with fifty children hanging on the van!)

14. *Balance your activities.* Do not expose people to everything on the first day. Stagger the events over the duration of your stay.

**Sample Itinerary**

The following itinerary is from a team that went to the Dominican Republic for ten days.

---

DAY 1: Travel to country; arrive in Puerta Plata and travel to Jacagua; settle into lodging; team meeting and orientation.

DAY 2: Work day (wake up 6:30 a.m.; breakfast 7:00; work site 8:00; lunch break noon to 3:00 p.m.; work site 3:00-5:30; dinner 6:30; team meeting 8:00).

DAY 3: Work day; evening meeting with local pastor to hear his story.

DAY 4: Sleep in! Travel to Jarabacoa to see falls; return to town for evening church service with nationals.

DAY 5: Work; evening meeting with missionaries to hear their story.

DAY 6: Work; team breaks into smaller groups and has dinner in a national's home.

DAY 7: Work in morning; city tour of Santiago with shopping opportunities; dinner in city; return for game night with local church.

DAY 8: Finish work and clean up area; say good-bys; depart for hotel outside of Puerta Plata; swim/relax.

DAY 9: Morning final shopping opportunities; afternoon at the beach (snorkeling available); dinner in Puerta Plata; final team meeting.

DAY 10: Depart for home midafternoon.

---

## TEAM ITINERARY

Use this space to make notes about your initial plans for work, rest, worship, and play. As plans develop or change, keep careful written notes on the blank pages at the back of the book.

| DAY | EVENT | ARRANGEMENTS |
|-----|-------|--------------|
|     |       |              |

## ESTABLISHING A PER PERSON PRICE FOR THE TEAM

Counting the costs—where do you begin? Setting the price can be a daunting task given the many variables: fluctuating airline prices, emergency funds, food budgets, lodging costs, and so on. If you are working with an agency, they may establish the cost for you. But if you're working alone, the place to begin is with the VWAP set-up sheet (see page 52). Once that sheet is completed, you will know where you will lodge, who will provide the food, project funds needed, and much other budgetary information. Next, contact a travel agent to find out what seasonal or group discounts may apply. Even though you are planning early, see if you can get a fairly concrete idea of what airline fares will be. Do you plan to rent ground transportation as well? Contact rental companies who operate in the area. (Note: Most rental car companies will not allow you to take vehicles rented in the United States very far into Mexico. Be sure you know each company's policy.)

Once you have gathered the necessary information, use the chart on the next page to establish the per person cost. (Another copy is included on page 209.) It is better to overestimate your cost by about 20 percent so you definitely have enough to cover expenses. Since it is unfair to ask team members for more money in the field, the leadership needs to establish with the mission agency who will be responsible for additional emergency costs (e.g., the church or the mission agency).

## COST PER PERSON

### GROUP COSTS

| | |
|---|---|
| Printing | $_____ |
| Postage | $_____ |
| Ground Transportation | $_____ |
| Lodging*** | $_____ |
| Project Materials | $_____ |
|    Total Group Costs | $_____ (1) |
|    Number of Team Members | _____ (2) |
| Average Cost Per Team Member (1 ÷ 2) | $_____ (3) |

### INDIVIDUAL COSTS

| | |
|---|---|
| Airline* | $_____ |
| All Meals** | $_____ |
| Lodging*** | $_____ |
| Country Tax | $_____ |
| Touring Costs | $_____ |
| Mission Agency Fee | $_____ |
|    Total Individual Cost | $_____ (4) |
|    Total Per Person Cost (3 + 4) | $_____ |

*Check with airline; it is possible that one or more may fly free.
**Includes "project" and R & R portions.
***May be individual or group, depending on accommodations.

Team members usually appreciate the chance to pay their costs in installments. Before setting arbitrary deadlines, fill in the spaces below to make sure you will have enough funds to pay the major expenses as they arise.

| EXPENSE | DATE DUE | AMOUNT |
| --- | --- | --- |
| Pay Airfare: | | |
| Mission Agency Fees: | | |
| Hotel Deposit: | | |

By this point in your planning process, you may feel somewhat overwhelmed at what seems like a mountain of details. People at your church may be very excited as they watch the plans beginning to unfold, yet they haven't known how they can help or otherwise be involved.

The next step presents you with the opportunity to share your dream with others and invite them to be a part of making the VWAP happen!

CHAPTER EIGHT

# SELECTING YOUR TEAM

**Sample Bulletin Announcement**

> There will be a Vacations with a Purpose team leaving for Guatemala on Saturday, June 23. All who are interested should be at the airport by 9:00 a.m. with a passport, $1,500, and a willing spirit. For those not able to join us, please keep the team in your prayers.

Would you want to lead this team? Probably not. You'd have no idea who would be on it. You need a selection process!

What are the best ways to select people for your team? Team selection involves a number of stages and requires from two to four weeks. In this section, we will cover who should select the team, the informational meeting, the application process, the application deposit, the participant interview, and the issue of references.

## STEP ONE: WHO SELECTS THE TEAM?

The team leader may feel uncomfortable with the sole responsibility for selecting or rejecting applicants who are his or her peers. Furthermore, since the process is subjective, it is best not to have just one person make the decisions.

However, it also may become an unwieldy process if left to a committee. A large selection committee representing many areas of the church is a cumbersome vehicle for decision making. Yet, since the team will be sent as "ambassadors" of the church or group, various church leaders may want a say in who goes on the team.

In the introduction to part 2, we advised that no matter what type of committee structure you develop for running your VWAP, one person should be designated the liaison between the team leader and the church. We have found that a small "selection committee" comprised of the staff liaison and the team leader(s) facilitates the team selection process. Discuss the possibilities with your planning team and decide how team selection might best be accomplished in your group.

## STEP TWO: RECRUITING YOUR TEAM

To receive applications, you have to get the word out about the opportunity. Even though we have organized numerous teams in our own groups, we find that each trip has to be promoted as though it were the first trip. It is important to understand some of the barriers people face when making a decision to apply.

- Fear of the unknown: foreign travel, foreign language, foreign diseases.
- Misconceptions about missions. (Many people hold a narrow view of what missions are and what missionaries do. They do not feel they fit into this narrow view.)
- Viewing these kinds of trips as only for "super Christians."
- The cost of the trip.
- Getting time off work.

Ideas for promoting your team are shown below. In light of the barriers outlined above, be sure to cover the following points:

- Allay travel concerns by communicating the logistics and the relative safety people feel when traveling as a group.
- People don't have to be missionaries or even inclined toward lifetime mission service to participate in this trip.
- Team members are "ordinary" Christians; you don't have to be a spiritual giant to sign up.
- Fund-raising opportunities are available to help potential team members meet the financial obligations of the trip.
- In addition, be sure to capitalize on the positive issues cited in chapter 1 that make a VWAP so appealing to many of today's adults (see page 15).

### SUGGESTIONS FOR PROMOTION

### Information Flyer
It helps tremendously to put all the important information on one sheet of paper or in an attractive brochure that people can take home and look over. This also eliminates having to answer many of the same questions over and over again. Here is a list of information the sheet should include:

- Country description
- Project description
- Housing arrangements
- Price of the VWAP, and what is included
- Other things the team will do or see

- Application procedure and deadline
- Phone number to call with questions

Following is a sample of what one group used to promote a trip to Mexico City.

---

### MEXICO CITY TEAM, JULY 20 TO AUGUST 5, JALAPA

*Country:* The team will be in Mexico City, the largest city in the world with 21 million inhabitants. It is a city rich in Mexican history and culture, but it is also a city plagued with intense poverty and need. Team participants will have the opportunity to experience firsthand the various aspects of the city. The project will focus on a community center designed to minister to the poorest of the poor. Team members will be struck by the great need in this area, and they will get an opportunity to touch and be touched by the people in significant ways.

*Project:* During the five days of work, the team will be doing construction on a building currently used for a variety of community services, including children's programming, nutritional training, and as a store with used clothing and toys. By helping to complete the roof and do other work, the team will help make possible further services to the community, such as medical care. In addition, the team will help with some of the current programming at the community center (work in the store, do puppet shows, and mime for the children, etc.). No specific skills are required or necessary, just a *big* desire to serve and be available. Be prepared to meet a lot of children!

*Other Activities:* Other activities will include experiencing the Mexican culture, history, and of course, food! The team will visit the fabulous Folklore Ballet at the National Palace of Fine Arts and the ruins at Teotihuacan. The week will end with two days shopping and touring in the Zona Rosa section of Mexico City.

*Accommodations:* Team members will stay in groups of two or three with Mexican families in a different section of the city from where they are working. There will be many of the conveniences of home, such as electricity and showers. Many of the people know some English, so don't let a lack of speaking Spanish keep you from participating. Two nights will be spent in a hotel in Mexico City.

*Cost:* In addition to the $795 cost (subject to adjustment because of airfare rate hikes, strikes, or changes in carrier), each team member must raise $100 for construction costs. Price includes: round-trip air travel from Tampa, transportation in country, all meals (except when touring), departure taxes, and lodging.

*Application Deadline:* Completed applications must be received no later than May 1. A $100 nonrefundable, nontransferable deposit is required with the application (if application is not accepted, deposit will be refunded). Since space is limited to fifteen people, acceptance will largely depend on the earliest applications and deposits received. (Trip conducted by Single Purpose Ministries.)

❖  ❖  ❖

## Slide/Video Presentation

If possible, present a brief and fast-moving slide or video presentation. There is no need to show every aspect of the country and/or project.

One group sets the slides from former VWAP trips to the music of a popular song. The lyrics often deal with people making a difference in the world around them. The slide show causes people to see themselves as participants.

## Testimonies from People Who Have Gone Before

In your recruiting, utilize testimonials from former participants who are good communicators. When possible, use people who have something in common with their audience. For example, if you are promoting an opportunity to adults in their twenties and thirties, arrange for testimonies from individuals in that age range. When the potential applicants hear the testimony of someone with whom they identify, they are more likely to overcome the perception that the trip is not for them. After your first team returns, this will be your most effective promotional tool.

## Word of Mouth

The team leader's own enthusiasm for the upcoming trip is another good promotional tool. Team leaders (and former team members) can make phone calls or initiate conversations with people in their social circle. The credibility and respect they command sometimes has a greater impact than slides and brochures.

## Informational Meeting

Hold an informational meeting about one month before the final deadline for applications. The purpose of this meeting is twofold: to explain the trip's details to those interested in participating, and to interview prospective team members. With peoples' busy schedules, individual interviews are hard to manage, so a gathering of possible participants is really a must. Show slides or a video of the country and project if you have them. Discuss the expectations for team participation and the financial obligations of team members. Allow for a question/answer session.

## STEP THREE: THE APPLICATION PROCESS

We highly recommend using an application process for team selection. Applications yield essential information: the person's skills, experience, and background. They are useful, not only in selecting members, but also in informing the hosts of who is coming.

In the forms section on pages 207-208, you will find an application that can be copied for use by your team. Feel free to adapt it to your particular church or organization.

Once the applications are turned in and a team member is accepted, make a copy of the application for each of the team leaders. The leader(s) should carry these applications with other team information. We also recommend sending copies to the agency personnel on the field, as this will help familiarize them with the team and its skills.

The application in form 1 is divided into three sections, each of which provides important information for selecting the team.

Part 1 asks for basic biographical information. The request for a birth date is important for selecting intergenerational teams. Try to have more than one representative from each age group if possible (a twenty-two-year-old may feel uncomfortable on a team made up solely of people her parents' age).

Part 2 tells you the particular skills around which you may be able to form your team.

Part 3 is vital in learning each person's background, Christian commitment, and motives for making the trip.

Note: What you do with the information in part 3 is up to you. People whose motive for applying is to "help the poor, primitive natives who have nothing" may be naive. But they may benefit greatly from participating, as well as make a significant contribution to the team. "Teachability" can be more important than naive motives.

## What to Watch for on Applications

*Medical Problems:* Would a person with special medical needs create difficulties on the VWAP? Would you need to make special provisions for the person? Issues may include dietary restrictions, physical limitations, and necessary medications.

*Wrong Motivations:* Does the application indicate that the person is motivated by reasons which conflict with the VWAP goals? For example, is the person looking to escape some major problem at home (e.g., broken relationship, job loss, death in family)? Is the person going because he or she wants to be with someone who is on the team? Is he or she just looking for an opportunity to travel? (One team member on a European VWAP created problems by pestering the leader to visit a major tourist attraction. She eventually left the team to do the sightseeing she had planned on!)

*Financial Difficulties:* This and potential trouble getting time off work are problems that should be self-explanatory.

*Negative Experiences on a Previous Team:* If the applicant states previous short-term mission experience, contact the previous team leader to find out if there were any difficulties. Contact references and read any evaluations that may be on file. A previously negative experience does not necessarily preclude a person's participation, but be sure to talk together and help the person think through the negative reactions to the last trip. How will these reactions affect the next endeavor?

*Emotional or Psychological Difficulties:* These problems may not surface on the application, but they must be addressed. The interview process and referral to references can help expose psychological and emotional difficulties. Occasionally it is necessary to refuse an applicant on the basis of conditions diagnosed as problematic or detrimental to the well-being of all concerned (e.g., kleptomania, sociopathy, suicidal behavior). However, we have allowed persons to go who were considered socially awkward, difficult, or immature by many who knew them. In this situation, the team leader and church leaders must agree that the potential harm the person might bring the team and the host community is far outweighed by the possible benefit to the applicant. The "inconvenience" of having this person on the team is minor compared to the possibilities for personal growth and development.

## Application Fee

We suggest you require a nonrefundable deposit upon acceptance to the team. Cash on the barrel head causes people to become serious about participation. In these days of "holding out for better options," the deposit is the team member's commitment to you (and to himself!) to follow through. A nonrefundable deposit is also preventive medicine for the ulcers that can develop in planning for an unknown quantity of participants. (Note: The deposit is generally equal to the amount of money that will be lost if the person decides not to make the trip. For example: the penalty for canceling or changing an airline reservation.)

## STEP FOUR: INTERVIEWS AND REFERENCES

The purpose of the interview is to ascertain whether or not the applicant will learn and grow from the experience and to ensure that his or her participation will not be detrimental to the team. This is also the time to look at "wrong" motivations. Are they due to a lack of exposure to VWAP goals? Or do they come from deeply held views that will negatively affect the experience of others? Because applications cannot reveal everything, interviews are strongly suggested for selecting your team.

Interviews can be arranged individually or as part of the informational meeting described previously. For the latter, ask people to bring a completed application to the informational meeting. After the question/answer period, have the selection committee sit down with one or two prospective team members for a more in-depth conversation.

To learn more about the interested person, ask if he or she has further questions. The type of questions the person asks may offer insight into motives for participating and his or her capacity to assimilate the many experiences of the trip. In addition, other helpful information may include the person's prior travel experience, reaction to adversity, attitudes about unusual or uncomfortable situations, and experience living in close contact with others for several days or weeks. Interviews of this nature enable you to identify those applicants who may have a negative or detrimental effect on the team.

The selection committee may not always know the people applying for the trip. In this case, we strongly suggest asking for references. When possible, references should be people who are known and respected in your church or ministry. When contacting references, explain the purposes and objectives of the VWAP. Describe travel conditions, group living situations, and other potentially difficult situations. Ask the contact if he or she has any concerns about the applicant's participation on the trip. Is he a team player? Is she open and enthusiastic? What does the contact know about the person's faith? Questions like these eliminate some of the unknown factors that might present problems later.

## STEP FIVE: INVOLVING OTHERS IN YOUR TEAM

Selecting participants is only the beginning of building a team. Many others who are not traveling to the host community can be a part of the "team" as well.

One evening we were meeting in a restaurant with a Canadian group that was preparing to go on a VWAP to Haiti. As we stood in the waiting area, the team leader apologized that the majority of the team was late. He assured us they'd all be along at any time.

Shortly, the rest of the team arrived in one large group. I heard the team leader ask one of the team members how Bill was doing. The team member, Greg, said Bill was doing well and had appreciated the visit. Curious, I asked if Bill was a member of the team. "Well, yeah," said Greg, "I guess he really is. He's a friend of mine who was paralyzed in a farming accident. He's come to all of our team meetings but couldn't come tonight because he's fighting bedsores from his wheelchair. We all stopped by his place for a cup of coffee before the meeting." Greg later explained that the entire trip would be videotaped since Bill's quadriplegia would prevent him from traveling with the team to Haiti.

As this group from British Columbia demonstrated, there are many creative ways to invite others to be part of the team. Some good ideas are explained here:

Once the team completes form 4 found on page 211, the team leader gives it to prayer partners who remain anonymous until the team returns home. During the trip these prayer partners pray for their particular team member. After returning, team members are matched with their prayer partners. Team members often show their appreciation by bringing a souvenir as a gift of thanks.

Chapter 9 lists several ideas for involving others in fund-raising (see pages 78-79).

Remember to involve others in the team preparation sessions to teach language, culture, history, and so on.

Ask volunteers to drive the team to and from the airport or to act as an emergency contact person. On one occasion, a person volunteered to stay by her phone on the days the team traveled so that if any team members got separated they would be able to contact someone who could help them by relaying messages back and forth.

## STEP SIX: COMMISSIONING THE TEAM

After the team has been selected, and sometime before they leave on the trip, the whole group should be brought before the congregation to be commissioned. The book of Acts describes how all ministers, missionaries, and even financial gifts from particular congregations were commissioned for service by the laying on of hands by the elders (Acts 6:6). We follow this example by asking those about to embark on a mission or other ministry to stand before the congregation and receive prayer and commissioning from a representative number of pastors, elders, and other interested church members and friends.

After you have completed these steps, you will have identified the team—not just those who will make the trip, but also those who will join you with their prayer and logistical support. In the next chapter, we'll explore the ways you can involve others in the financial support of your VWAP.

# FINANCING THE TEAM

It can be exciting to watch your team forming, to see the pieces falling into place . . . but somewhere, nagging in the back of your mind, is the fear of not raising enough funds. If we all had millions of dollars, we wouldn't need this chapter. But if we had all the money we ever needed, we wouldn't have the opportunity to see God's faithful providence at work! Financing this team and its projects will stretch your faith, as well as that of your team members and the entire local community. In fact, if financing the trip isn't a faith-stretching experience for all involved, then perhaps your sights are set too low!

This chapter is meant to assist you in the overall leadership of the fund raising for the team. The team member's manual (chapter 3, beginning on page 31) contains most of the information you will see below. If team members are going to raise funds individually, we recommend you take time at a team meeting to go through their material and add any necessary comments. If team members are raising funds as a group, skim this for the pertinent information.

## SENDING LETTERS

One of the best ways to raise funds is by personally asking people to support you in the VWAP experience. Many team members have told us that, even though they were initially put off by the idea of sending support letters, it turned into one of the best aspects of the whole adventure. An avid football fan from one team wrote the head coach of his favorite college football team in the Big Ten Conference. His letter explained the purpose of the trip, his hopes and goals, and described the need. The coach, who had never met this young man, sent a check for $250! Another woman sent a letter to the owner of a company that does a lot of business with the firm where she works. Not only did he make a very large donation to the team, but he was very interested in hearing about her experience when she returned.

There are three types of support letters. Discuss the fund-raising plan with each team member and help him or her decide which type(s) of letter would be most appropriate.

1. *Letter sent out by the team member requesting funds for his or her trip.*
2. *Letter sent out requesting funds for the project.* If team members decide to pay for their own trip, they may still wish to ask for donations for the project itself. In this case, team members will explain in the letter that they are paying their own costs but are asking friends to contribute toward the project.
3. *Letter requesting prayer but no money.* Even if you do not need any funds, we encourage you to have team members include others in their VWAP by inviting people to pray for the endeavor.

## GUIDELINES FOR FUND-RAISING LETTERS

Team members who are raising funds for their own participation may consider sending letters to friends, business associates, relatives, and others.

1. Information about the country/culture they are going to. Include a brief description of the area and things such as per capita income, literacy rate, population, etc.
2. Information on the sending organization and the hosting organization. The sending organization is the church or ministry planning the trip. The hosting group is the mission agency and/or national church with whom you are working.
3. Description of what the team will be doing. Include why the team is doing this particular project. For example, if the team is building a rural clinic, why is that a need in the host community?
4. The cost of the trip.
5. Why the person wants to be involved in this trip. Have the team member briefly list his or her strongest reasons for going on this trip. He or she may mention a desire to become more globally aware and develop a deeper faith. But readers would be more likely to donate money to an actual project or activity they can see.
6. How team members would like the reader to be involved. They need to address why they are asking people to contribute financially. Have them go back to the project description mentioned in the third guideline and ask the reader to support this endeavor by contributing to the specific expenses the team incurs by going. This need not be a long "sales pitch" but rather a simple request.
7. Clear instructions on how contributors are to respond, including:

   • Who to make the check payable to (checks should not be made payable to the team member if the contributor wishes the donation to be tax-deductible);
   • Where to mail it;
   • When you need it;
   • Whether the team member is requesting prayer, financial assistance, or both.

Have each team member compose his or her own letter. People prefer to read a personalized letter as opposed to a form letter that is sent by everyone on the team.

Also, stress that he or she *keep it brief.* The first page will probably be read; others may not be.

The team member's manual has pages for recording information about how much the trip and project will cost, due dates for payments, and a record of donors (page 35 in team member's manual). Discuss this information regularly. Team leaders have often told us they feel uncomfortable asking their team members about finances. Be assured that this awkwardness is one-sided. The team members realize that raising money and making their payments is part of their preparation. The section below will help you feel more confident about leading your team through the fund-raising.

## LEADER'S ROLE DURING FUND-RAISING

1. Review all fund-raising ideas *before* they are implemented. By doing this you help to ensure that the integrity of your VWAP program is not compromised. You may also add valuable insight into the implementation of an idea, thus helping to ensure its success.
2. Regularly monitor how each team member's finances are coming in. Establish deadlines and keep to them. Some people have a tendency to put things off, and this can complicate things if you have airline bills to pay! By monitoring team members' progress, you will be better able to encourage those who need it and affirm those who are doing well.
3. Run the funds through the church. Do not run donations through your own account or through the accounts of individual team members. In many situations, funds given to VWAP are tax-deductible. Check with the treasurer of the church to see if this is the case and how he or she wants you to handle the collection and distribution of the funds.
4. Bring the entire group into the fund-raising endeavor. This VWAP experience should be owned by the group/church as a whole. If the entire congregation is a part of the fund-raising, they will be more interested and enthusiastic about your team's experience. As individual team members share their enthusiasm, more people become involved through prayer and support. In turn, the awareness and concern for missionaries and the broader church family grows far beyond the team itself. Since much of the support for these teams will come from unchurched friends and colleagues, including others in fund-raising provides team members with great opportunities to share their faith and concern for the world once they've returned.
5. Encourage those not raising personal support to raise project funds through support letters. Some may feel uncomfortable sending letters asking people to contribute to them personally, but they may not feel uncomfortable asking people to contribute to a school building or clinic supplies.

6. Let team members know from the start exactly what the costs are and what they are responsible for.

## GROUP FUND-RAISING IDEAS

Several suggestions for raising funds are listed below (and in the team member's manual, chapter 3, pages 33-34). You undoubtedly have other ideas of your own. In addition, your public library or church library may have information on the subject. Keep a detailed record of the ideas you use and how successful they are. This record will help in the planning for future teams.

### Fun Runs

One large urban church has raised more than $35,000 in scholarships and project costs for the past four years by sponsoring a 10K run/5K walk each spring. The event attracts people of all ages from throughout the congregation. Funds are raised by runners/walkers, who seek sponsors for their participation, and by charging an entry fee to the more serious runners who like running in this officially timed race. This annual event now has the entire congregation involved in the idea and excitement of Vacations with a Purpose.

### Work Days

In another group, participants ask people to sponsor them for their work in some community project. The participant provides eight hours of labor to an organization like Habitat for Humanity or at the home of an elderly or disabled neighbor. Again, in addition to funds raised, the participant has the chance to share his or her enthusiasm for the upcoming VWAP.

### Food Fast

On an individual basis, team members and other supporters can skip one meal a week for a certain number of weeks and give the amount ($5) they would normally spend on the food toward the project.

### Activities

Plan an event and direct a percentage of the gate receipts toward the project. Design and sell T-shirts or visors promoting the trip. Offer special services around holidays. For example, team members could deliver singing telegrams, balloons, valentines, flowers, or home-made cakes or candies. Contact business owners or social clubs and ask if they will consider donating a percentage from their own fund raisers or public relations events (e.g., fashion shows, dinners, tennis matches). The Boston Children's Museum donated scores of promotional digital watches to one team going to the Dominican Republic. Due in part to the increased visibility of celebrities working for global concerns, businesses seem more willing to contribute to relief efforts.

**Auction**
A church in New England conducted an auction for their young adult ministry's summer VWAP. People donated their services to be auctioned off—everything from "cleaning out your refrigerator" to "a gourmet meal for four." After two weeks of soliciting services from the group, the auctioning began. This event raised over $3,000 for their team!

### IDEAS USED BY THIS TEAM

List your fund-raising ideas here as a record, but be sure to carefully document the specifics elsewhere so you can pass them along to the next team.

## PAYMENT DEADLINES

It may be difficult for team members to pay for the entire cost at once. A more reasonable approach is to collect the money in installments, making sure you receive sufficient payments to cover your costs as they arise. (As we mention elsewhere, it is important to make sure team members keep to the schedule.) Use the example below as a guideline for figuring payment deadlines and amounts.

Let's say your trip will cost the participants $1,200 each of which approximately $600 is airfare. The suggested time frame for the payments is as follows:

- A nonrefundable deposit of $100 is due with the application, but will be returned to anyone not accepted for team participation.
- The second payment is $600, which is the cost of the airfare. Since the tickets in this example must be paid for thirty days prior to travel, this payment is due five weeks prior to departure.
- The final installment is the remaining amount, or $500. It is due one week prior to departure.

Plan your payment schedule according to the model above, then communicate the dates to your team members. Have them fill in the dates on page 35 of their manual.

| PAYMENT | DATE DUE | AMOUNT |
|---------|----------|--------|
| Deposit | | |
| Payment 2 | | |
| Payment 3 | | |

# PART THREE
# PREPARING TO GO

*In part 2 we explored the process of identifying the people, places, and plans that make up Vacations with a Purpose. In part 3 you will be given tools and information to help prepare team members for the trip they are about to take.*

# CHAPTER TEN

# PREPARING YOUR TEAM

Team preparation is perhaps the most crucial portion of the VWAP experience. It is where the "purpose" behind the vacation is communicated. It is what instills the sense of *team* in each of the members.

## GOALS OF THE TEAM PREPARATION COURSE

The curriculum presented here is designed to meet the goals outlined below. Be sure to keep these goals in mind as you prepare your team. If you customize the curriculum for your group, be sure the changes are in accordance with these goals. As you select guest speakers with various areas of expertise, review the goals with them.

- The course will communicate to the members that they are a team. It defines what teamwork is and how it works in the VWAP context.
- The course heightens the team's awareness of the other culture. It illuminates the team members' perceptions of the other culture as well as their own.
- It prepares everyone to enter the host culture as a servant. It communicates the importance of learning and serving.
- It eases the burden of the hosts. It provides enough information to lessen the likelihood of embarrassing and harmful cultural gaffes. It provides the team members with the motivation and tools to communicate with nationals.
- It assists team members in preparing for the spiritual implications of the experience. It creates an expectancy and teachability toward God. They are going on a trip to learn about others, but their experience will teach much about themselves and the God they serve.

## HOW TO USE THIS CURRICULUM

Before your first session, make sure you become thoroughly familiar with the material in this chapter and in the appendix section at the back of the book (pages 183-204). For your convenience, each preparatory session includes the necessary material. As you prepare each session, ask yourself the following questions:

- Who can I invite to teach a particular session?
- What material is not included here that is necessary for this team?
- How can I make the sessions fun and interesting?
- How can I involve the team members during the sessions?

This curriculum is designed for six weekly sessions. Each session includes language instruction and two or more of the other building blocks. Each session ends with prayer, either as a group or in pairs. Sessions are designed to be from two to two-and-a-half hours in length. Team members are expected to complete all the homework for each session. Leaders should complete the team member assignments as part of their own preparation.

- If team members did not receive a copy of the *Vacations with a Purpose Team Member's Manual* upon acceptance to the team, make sure they obtain a copy before the beginning of the first session.
- Be sure to have a plan for getting the information to team members who have to miss a meeting due to unavoidable circumstances.
- This course is designed to be thorough, yet generic enough for all teams. Keep in mind that you can customize any portion of it to address needs that are particular to your group or to take advantage of the special gifts and talents of people who may be available. Be creative!

## CURRICULUM BUILDING BLOCKS

Visualize the team preparation course as a foundation on which the VWAP is built. The foundation is constructed, layer by layer, out of six types of building blocks. These blocks prepare your team in the areas of *cross-cultural awareness, team dynamics, language, personal preparation, logistics,* and *host country overview*. To this foundation, you may add miscellaneous topics that suit the needs of your team. The block foundation is held together with the mortar of prayer, an essential part of each team meeting. Each building block is described in the next several pages.

The team preparation course is an excellent place to use the resources you have available in your church or group. Seek out those people who can share from their experiences. Call on the talents of former missionaries, former VWAP team members, foreign exchange students, people who have traveled abroad for business or school, or members of the pastoral staff who have expertise in interpersonal relations or missions. Be creative. Look at the Body of Christ around you; God has gifted each one for the equipping of the saints. This course will be greatly enhanced by the involvement of others.

## ■ Building Block 1: Cross-Cultural Awareness

How often have you heard people returning from a vacation abroad complain that "people over there don't do things right!" This attitude can be fatal to the VWAP experience. Not only will it prevent your team members from gleaning many of the important lessons, but it can be very detrimental to the efforts of the missionaries working in the host's community. Plan this portion of the curriculum carefully. Utilize those people around you who are experienced in cross-cultural interaction.

## ■ Building Block 2: Team Dynamics

Teamwork will be crucial to the success of the team. A Vacation with a Purpose is *not* a collection of individuals merely going to a country to do some work. Rather, it is a group of individuals who are coming together to create an environment where they are able to work, learn, and grow together. This cannot be emphasized too strongly or too often. When relationships between team members are healthy, each person has the optimal chance to absorb all that a trip like this can teach. The New Testament is clear that interpersonal relationships affect how God is able to communicate with us and how our gifts and service are received by Him (Matthew 5:23-24).

## ■ Building Block 3: Language

The language portion of the course should aim to encourage everyone and intimidate no one. Many people have attempted language learning and found the experience harrowing. The key is to provide lighthearted, practical instruction that will leave team members with just a few phrases they can use confidently with the nationals they meet.

It goes without saying that four or six lessons of language instruction will not produce a team of bilinguals! The goal of this portion of the class is twofold: to help the team members learn that they don't need to be intimidated by a foreign language; and to accustom their ears to some of the words and phrases they're likely to hear. Each team member may have his or her own expectations of the language class: some may want to brush up on old high school skills, some may want to learn one or two phrases, some may simply want to hear and pronounce non-English words for the first time in their lives. The chief concerns of the language teacher should be that all students enjoy the class and that anxieties surrounding foreign language are minimized.

The curriculum found in chapter 11 (chapter 5 of team member's manual) is the same one we've used to teach teams going to Spanish-speaking countries. We have adapted it for use with whatever language you will be using on your trip. All you have to provide is an instructor. Ask someone who is familiar with the language you'll be using to use his or her own skills and background to adapt this material for your group's use.

This material can be used effectively without overwhelming the team. Since there are many excellent pocket phrase books and small, computerized translators available on the market, we have included only phrases specific to the church community.

# An Overview of the Six-Session Team Preparation Course

Here's a look at what your team will be doing to prepare for its missions trip.

| Session | Goal/Objective | Cross-Cultural Awareness | Team Dynamics |
|---|---|---|---|
| **Session One**<br><br>Day:_____<br><br>Date:_____ | Introduce team members to each other. Discuss the importance of teamwork. Give an overview of the trip. Discuss financial obligations. Begin language studies. | Use the "All About Me" exercise as a way of introducing teammates to one another. *20 minutes* **L: 91** | Go through the "Teamwork Factor" exercise. *30 minutes* **L: 91-93; T: 37-39** |
| **Session Two**<br><br>Day:_____<br><br>Date:_____ | Team members begin to learn about the country/region and explore their own preparedness for their Vacation with a Purpose. | | |
| **Session Three**<br><br>Day:_____<br><br>Date:_____ | Examine cross-cultural issues and stereotypes. Team members also continue to explore their personal goals for this VWAP. | Review the assigned selection called "Being a Bridge Builder." *30 minutes* **L: 103-106; T: 49-53** | |
| **Session Four**<br><br>Day:_____<br><br>Date:_____ | Learn more about the host country and/or important cross-cultural issues. As in prior sessions, language and logistics are addressed. (Note: Depending on the resource people you have available, select only the "Cross-Cultural" option or the "Host Country" option. Do not attempt to squeeze both into one session.) | (Choose between the "Host Country" and the "Cross-Cultural" options.) Invite a missionary to address cultural sensitivities, differences in value systems, etc. *40 minutes* **L: 109** | |
| **Session Five**<br><br>Day:_____<br><br>Date:_____ | Take a field trip to build team relationships and/or understand more about our own culture and values and what they say about how we view others. Focus on developing the attitude of a servant. | | Take one of two suggested field trips. Reconvene and discuss findings. Review "Being a Servant" exercise and discuss findings from last week's assignment. *60-80 minutes* **L: 113; T: 57** |
| **Session Six**<br><br>Day:_____<br><br>Date:_____ | Finalize all details surrounding actual travel and preparation for work project. | | |

**Where to find MORE DETAILS AND DIRECTIONS:**
The **L** indicates page numbers in the Leader's Manual; **T**, the Team Member's

| Language (Chapter 11) | Personal Preparation | Logistics | Host Country Overview | Assignments/ Prayer Topics |
|---|---|---|---|---|
| Help the team become accustomed to hearing and making new sounds. *40 minutes* **L: 118; T: 62** | | Establish team policies and guidelines. Discuss finances, due dates for each payment, fund-raising, passports, visas etc. *45 minutes* **L: 94-95; T: 44-45** | | Complete personal preparation worksheet. Assign team members to learn about host country/region. Draft letters to potential supporters. *Prayer topic: Team unity.* **L: 96-99; T: 39-43** |
| Help the team see that they probably know more foreign language than they think. *40 minutes* **L: 119; T: 63** | Review/discuss team's answers to personal preparation worksheet. Explore potential problem areas in their personal preparation. *30 minutes* **L: 96-99; T: 39-43** | Cover medical issues and precautions. Discuss specific items and preparation necessary for team project. *30 minutes* **L: 100-102; T: 46-48** | Have teams (chosen during the last session) give reports on what they found out about the host country/region. (See assignments column at right, session 1.) *30-40 minutes* | Read selection entitled "Being a Bridge Builder." Complete personal goals work-sheet. *Prayer topic: Personal preparation.* **L: 103-107; T: 49-53** |
| Begin to build a vocabulary and get basic understanding of the grammar. *40 minutes* **L: 120; T: 64** | Break into groups of three to discuss personal goals. Use accompanying goals worksheet as tool when praying for and encouraging team members. *20 minutes* **L: 107; T: 53** | Review each member's financial situation. Make final plans for tool or clothing drives, if applicable. Assign team medic, team mechanic, team photographer, etc. *30 minutes* | | Fill out prayer partner form. Complete "Release of Liability" form. *Prayer topic: Host community.* **L: 211-212;** |
| Be able to introduce oneself and give a brief personal description. *40 minutes* **L: 121-122; T: 65-66** | | Discuss the packing list and packing tips. *30 minutes* **L: 110-111; T: 54-56** | (Choose between the "Host Country" and "Cross-Cultural" options.) Invite a speaker who has lived in or frequently visited the country/region you will be visiting. *40 minutes* **L: 109** | Have team review the selection entitled "Being a Servant." *Prayer topic: The needs of the missionaries the team will work with.* **L: 113; T: 57** |
| Be able to ask others something about themselves in their language. *40 minutes* **L: 123-124; T: 67** | | Review team member finances. Discuss the importance of journaling. *30 minutes* | | Write thank-you notes to donors. *Prayer topic: The sending church.* **L: 114** |
| Help build team's confidence that they now know at least a few phrases that can be used in several situations. *40 minutes* **L: 125; T: 68-69** | | Review all final details including when and where to meet for flight. Distribute emergency contact telephone numbers. Discuss any last-minute informa-tion. *45 minutes* | | Complete final prep-aration for specific work project(s). For example, if conducting a vacation Bible school in the host community, learn activ-ities and games from a school teacher that can be executed with minimal language skills. *Prayer topic: Travel.* **L: 116** |

### ■ Building Block 4: Personal Preparation

Much of the team's personal preparation can be done individually and discussed in class. There are exercises and lessons provided for use in the class sessions which will assist team members in preparing emotionally and spiritually.

### ■ Building Block 5: Logistics

Team members will arrive at each class with questions and concerns about travel, packing, shots, and so on. The logistical details that apply to all teams are found in the appendix section of this manual. Others, which pertain only to your team, may be added by you. The team leader should compile all necessary information and impart it clearly, in detail, and in a timely manner. Never make any assumptions about what your team members know about travel. Explain *everything*! (One bit of advice: Save the logistics for the latter part of the class; otherwise, the questions drag on and can cut into valuable time.)

### ■ Building Block 6: Host Country Overview

The depth of your instruction here depends on the resources available to you. At the very least, team members should be provided with as much information as one would find in an encyclopedia entry or a travel guide. If possible, bring in guests to speak about the political or religious history of the country. Perhaps someone in your church is versed in the economics of the region, or the plants and animals your group is likely to encounter. You honor the nationals and the missionaries when you have learned about their country or region prior to arrival.

### Miscellaneous Preparation

This is where your creativity comes out. Tailor a portion of the class to the specific requirements of your team. Teams have had guest speakers address topics such as Pentecostalism in Latin America, teaching dental hygiene in remote villages, and how-to classes for various construction techniques. Use your creativity to think of topics that may interest your group and utilize the resources you have.

## SESSION ONE—TEAM PLAYERS

**Goal**

In this session, we will introduce the team members to each other, discuss the importance of teamwork, give an overview of the trip, discuss financial obligations, and begin language studies. Note: The material here and in the team member's manual will be read and discussed over a six-week period. However, it is helpful to encourage team members to review all the material before the first week.

### ◆ Cross-Cultural

Go through the "All About Me" exercise as a way of introducing teammates to one another. (Suggested time: twenty minutes.)

"All About Me": Doug and Adele Calhoun, young adult ministers at Park Street Church in Boston, use the following game with their teams.

Break the team into pairs and have team members attempt to learn at least three things about the other person without using any verbal communication (e.g., draw pictures or use sign language). Then come together as a group and have partners share what they learned about each other. This is a great way for the team to experience the frustration they may feel on the field when they can't easily communicate with the host community.

### ◆ Team Dynamics

Using the instructions that follow, go through the "TEAMWORK FACTOR" exercise (found in chapter 4 of the team member's handbook, pages 37-39). (Suggested time: thirty minutes.)

Going around the room one at a time, have team members give a definition or example of the words that make out the acronym "TEAMWORK FACTOR." Then have them compile their own list of words that list the traits of a person who is not a team player. (For example, you might start with Stubborn, Elitist, Noncooperative.) Without telling them the solution, see if they can figure out that the acronym is "SEND ME HOME!"

### THE TEAMWORK FACTOR

Just what does teamwork mean? What are the traits of a team player? We have come up with fourteen words that form the basis of what we call the "TEAMWORK FACTOR," the traits exhibited by those who are pitching in to do their part for the good of the group.

## T is for Teachable

A teachable spirit helps create a noncompetitive environment in which learning and sharing come naturally. Teachability gives all members the freedom to make mistakes as they learn.

## E is for Encouraging

Think of how encouraging words enhance the development of a community. What differences do they make?

## A is for Appreciative

What things can we appreciate in others on the team? How can we show our appreciation?

## M is for Motivated

Take initiative! Do all things as unto the Lord! (Colossians 3:17,23).

## W is for Willing

Team members may have different levels of strength, skill, and health, but each should be willing to work to the best of his or her capabilities. Willingness also includes accepting uncomfortable conditions in the host country. Willingly take on the heat, food, bugs, and germs.

## O is for Open

Be open with what you are learning, experiencing, feeling, thinking, etc. Express both the positive and negative. Your vulnerability with others builds community.

## R is for Refreshing

The times may be tough—heat, sickness, exhaustion, physical labor, emotion drain, and so on. In those times it will be incredibly refreshing to have another team member help pick up your spirits! Think about how you can be replenishers to each other on a daily basis.

## K is for Kindred Spirit

There's a sense of camaraderie as we pursue this together. We are all part of the Christian family and we're all in this together!

## F is for Flexible

Anything can change from day to day. A flexible team member will learn to accept the unexpected as the norm.

## A is for Agreeable

Living together in close quarters, sharing crowded bathing facilities, and every other aspect of group travel requires everyone to be gracious.

## C is for Cooperative
Share with one another, help and assist one another. Instead of grumbling about problems, propose solutions!

## T is for Thoughtful
What can you do to make a teammate's day a little easier?

## O is for Obedient
There will be times when the team leader has to "pull rank" and make unpopular decisions. A team player will respect the leader's authority and encourage others to do the same.

## R is for Relational
Get to know the others on your team. Go out of your way to learn about their hopes, their dreams, their history.

Get the picture! The "TEAMWORK FACTOR" spells out the difference between a group of isolated individuals and a team of interconnected members.

Now it's your turn to compile your own list of negative traits, using the first letter shown in each space below. Think of words that work against community and destroy team spirit.

```
N
E
E
M
S
H
E
M
O
D
```

Now rearrange the letters to find out what you're saying to the team when you exhibit these traits:

___ ___ ___ ___   ___ ___   ___ ___ ___ ___!

(Answer: SEND ME HOME!)

❖  ❖  ❖

### ◆ Language

See session 1 found on page 118 of this manual and chapter 5, page 62, of the team member's manual. (Suggested time: forty minutes. Note: Each language session is planned for a forty-minute time slot.)

### ◆ Logistics

Below is a list of *team policies* used by one group. Use this covenant or create a similar set of guidelines and discuss it with the group during this session; have each team member sign it. (This statement is found in team member's manual, chapter 4, pages 44-45.) (Suggested time: forty-five minutes.)

---

### VWAP POLICY STATEMENT

I realize that the following elements are crucial to the effectiveness, quality, and safety of our trip together. As a member of this Vacations with a Purpose team, I agree to:

1. Remember that I am a guest working at the invitation of a local missionary, pastor, medical clinic, etc. If my hosts are offended by bare arms, shirtless backs, and exposed legs, I'll cover them. If they offer me goat meat stew, I'll try it! I'll remember the missionaries' prayer: "Where You lead me, I will follow; what You feed me, I will swallow!"

2. Remember that we have come to learn, not to teach. I may run across procedures that I feel are inefficient, or attitudes that I find closed minded. I'll resist the temptation to inform our hosts about "how we do things." I'll be open to learning about other people's methods and ideas.

3. Respect the host's view of Christianity. I recognize that Christianity has many faces throughout the world, and that the purpose of this trip is to witness and experience faith lived out in a new setting.

4. Develop and maintain a servant attitude toward all nationals and my teammates.

5. Respect my team leader(s) and his or her decisions.

6. Refrain from gossip. I may be surprised at how each person will blossom when freed from the concern that others may be passing judgment.

7. Refrain from complaining. I know that travel can present numerous unexpected and undesired circumstances, but the rewards of conquering such circumstances are innumerable. Instead of whining and complaining, I'll be creative and supportive.

8. Respect the work that is going on in the country with the particular church, agency, or person(s) that we are working with. I realize that our team is here for just a short while, but that the missionary and local church are here for the long term. I will respect their

knowledge, insights, and instructions.
9. Attend all team preparation classes and follow-up meetings.
10. Fulfill all logistical requirements. I will comply with all requirements regarding passports, finances, shots, and so on.
11. Refrain from negative political comments or hostile discussions concerning our host country's politics.
12. Remember not to be exclusive in my relationships. If my sweetheart or spouse is on the team, we will make every effort to interact with all members of the team, not just one another. If I am attracted to a teammate, I will not attempt to pursue an exclusive relationship until after we return home.
13. Refrain from any activity that could be construed as romantic interest toward a national. I realize certain activities that seem innocuous in my own culture may seem inappropriate in others.
14. Abstain from the consumption of alcoholic beverages or the use of tobacco or illegal drugs while on the trip.

Signed _____ Date _____

❖  ❖  ❖

Finances should be discussed during this session and often thereafter. Make sure the team members know the due dates for each payment and encourage them in their fund-raising. (See chapter 9 for more about this. Important information for team members is found in chapter 3 of their manuals, beginning on page 31.)

During the first meeting, establish which team members may not yet have passports (if necessary for your destination). Advise team members to apply for passports immediately. If visas are necessary, this should also be discussed during this session.

### ◆ Assignments
Each assignment is due the following session.

1. Complete personal preparation worksheet found below.
2. Assign pairs of team members the task of learning about the history, economy, politics, and religious issues of the host country/region. Suggest they find magazine articles, books, or someone with personal knowledge of the area.
3. Have team members draft letters to potential supporters.

### ◆ Prayer Topic
Team unity.

## PERSONAL PREPARATION

Preparation is a key ingredient for a successful and life-changing short-term missions experience. As the leader most of the preparation falls on you. It requires time and work. The following issues and questions will stimulate your thinking as well as that of the team members as you all prepare for the trip. (Material for team members is found in the team member's manual, chapter 4, pages 39-43.)

### Are You Prepared Physically?

1. Are you in shape? What exercises could you be doing to get in better shape for your particular project (e.g., walking, jogging, etc.)?

2. Are you in good health? What steps could you take to improve your health prior to the trip (e.g., diet, sleep, etc.)?

### Are You Prepared Emotionally?

3. Are you in shape emotionally? Think through the following questions.

   a. Are there any unresolved issues or relationships in your life?

   b. Are you having any bouts with depression or discouragement that should be talked out prior to your trip?

   c. Would it be wise to talk these out with a pastor, counselor, or friend?

d. Could you be viewing this trip as some sort of therapy for problems in your life?

e. If you are, what problems are you trying to "escape" from? Why?

## Are You Prepared Spiritually?

4. A mission trip is not the time to be getting things together with God. Instead, you should be developing and improving your relationship with Him now.

a. Reflect on where you are spiritually. What will give you a richer experience *if* you begin to do it now?

b. *Start listening:* Are you listening to God? Are there quiet times in your day to reflect on what God is teaching you?

c. *Start reading:* Are you spending time reading God's Word? How consistently?

d. *Start speaking:* What's your prayer life like? Are you taking time each day to talk with God?

e. *Start responding:* Are you striving to be obedient in the little things? Are you attempting to apply the things God is teaching you?

## Are You Prepared Relationally?

5. You will be spending much of your time with a group of people to whom your experience will be closely tied. Consequently, it is important to think through the way you relate interpersonally.

a. Are you prone to any types of conflict that hinder your ability to work with others? What are they? When are they most likely to occur?

b. Do you consider yourself a good listener? How might this be improved before joining the team?

c. Are you comfortable being transparent with others? What factors determine whether or not you will share with another? What obstacles do you have when it comes to being open and vulnerable?

d. Would you consider yourself to be a cooperative person? Why, or why not? Are there certain circumstances when you find it hard to be cooperative with others? What are they? Do group decisions frustrate you?

## Think Through Your Expectations
6. Write down your expectations for this trip in the space below.

7. Go back and make a check by the expectations that could be unrealistic. Why are they unrealistic?

8. How could they be adapted to become more realistic?

9. Have you ever been disappointed due to unrealistic expectations? Explain.

10. As you look over your expectations, what areas of potential disappointment do you see on this trip?

## SESSION TWO—INFORMED TRAVELERS

> **Goal**
> In this session, team members will begin to learn about the country/region and explore their own preparedness for their Vacation with a Purpose.

### ◆ Personal Preparation

Review and discuss the team's answers to the personal preparation worksheet. Lead a discussion with the entire group, or break them into smaller groups for self-led discussions. Discuss potential problem areas in their personal preparation. (Suggested time: thirty minutes.)

### ◆ Host Country

Have the pairs chosen during the last session give reports on what they found out about the host country. (Suggested time: thirty to forty minutes.)

### ◆ Language

See page 119 of this manual, and chapter 5, page 63, of the team member's manual.

### ◆ Logistics

(Suggested time: thirty minutes.)

1. Discuss the *medical precautions* found below. Be sure you or a team member researches the requirements for the area to which you will be traveling. The hosting agency, your mission pastor, or your local health department can help you.
2. Discuss specific items and preparation needed for project.
3. Mail support letters to potential sponsors. If team members have questions about the wording of their letter, review it with them.
4. Review itinerary.

### MEDICAL PRECAUTIONS

Important: We recommend that you consult your local health department or your host to see which shots and/or medication you may need for the area you will visit. Do you need to take precautions against such diseases as typhoid, malaria, and various types of gastric distress? In some cases, there is very minimal reason for concern. On the other hand, many countries require proof of vaccination before you may begin your travel. Be sure you check what applies in the area where you'll be.

In all cases, it is wise to have a current tetanus booster and a supply of Pepto Bismol or similar product for the prevention and/or relief of diarrhea.

## Health Guidelines

Duane (Chip) Anderson, a missionary with Latin American Mission in San Jose, Costa Rica, makes the following suggestions for team members traveling in his area. They seem to make sense for all teams traveling outside of North America. (Team members can find this information in chapter 4 of their manuals, pages 46-47.)

1. Be sure the water you drink is safe. Drink bottled water or purify tap water before drinking. Avoid ice cubes made from tap water; freezing does not kill the offending bacteria.
2. Avoid uncooked vegetables, salads, and fruit that cannot be peeled.
3. Do not eat raw eggs, uncooked meat, or unprocessed cheese.
4. Bring a container of hand towelettes, as washing facilities are not always available.
5. Take your customary medications along with a renewal prescription. Be sure to know the generic names of your prescribed drugs. Also, bring your prescription for eyeglasses. Notify your host and team leader of any special medical needs well before you arrive on the field.
6. When traveling in the tropics, be very careful of intense sun. Apply sunscreens and wear protective clothing.
7. Pepto Bismol is one of the most effective remedies to prevent and relieve diarrhea. Two tablespoons (or two tablets) is the recommended dosage. If vomiting accompanies diarrhea, refrain from food and drink for one hour, then try a tablespoon of clear liquid every five minutes for one hour.
8. *Notify the team leader and seek professional care* if any of the following occur:

   • diarrhea lasting more than seventy-two hours,
   • bloody diarrhea,
   • persistent or severe abdominal cramps or pain,
   • vomiting lasting more than six to twelve hours,
   • severe chills, and/or
   • painful urination or discharge.

(This material is adapted from "Short-Term Teams Leaders Guide," by Duane Anderson, Christ for the City, LAM, San Jose, Costa Rica, 1989.)

## Medical Insurance

Long before you leave, check with your private (or Canadian government) carrier to see if you will be covered by insurance while out of the country. If so, find out all the necessary details in case medical care is necessary. For example, will you have to pay out-of-pocket and get reimbursed when you return? What information will the insurance company require you to get while still at the clinic or hospital? Is there a phone number to call if you get hurt?

If you are not covered, check into getting a temporary travelers' policy.

These are generally inexpensive. Keep in mind that most missionary agencies require you to have medical coverage.

| SUGGESTED MEDICAL KIT | |
|---|---|
| ❑ Band-Aids® | ❑ aspirin |
| ❑ adhesive pads | ❑ Advil®/Tylenol® |
| ❑ sterile pads | ❑ Pepto Bismol®/Kaopectate® |
| ❑ Ace Bandage® | ❑ throat lozenges |
| ❑ hydrogen peroxide | ❑ rubbing alcohol |
| ❑ thermometer | ❑ Benadryl Cream® |
| ❑ Ben-Gay® | ❑ Neosporin® |
| ❑ scissors | ❑ cotton balls |
| ❑ cold medications | ❑ moist towelettes |
| ❑ adhesive tape | ❑ Immodium® |
| ❑ laxative | ❑ Lomotil® (prescription) |
| ❑ tweezers | ❑ antibiotics |

❖ ❖ ❖

◆ **Assignment**
1. Read the following section entitled "Being a Bridge Builder." (Session 3, pages 49-54, in team member's manual.)
2. Complete the personal goals worksheet, which follows next section. (Session 3, page 53, in team member's manual.)

◆ **Prayer Topic**
Personal preparation.

## SESSION THREE—BRIDGE BUILDERS

> **Goal**
> In this session, we will examine cross-cultural issues and stereotypes. Team members will also continue to explore their goals for this VWAP.

### ◆ Cross-Cultural

Review the assigned section called "Being a Bridge Builder." (Team members can find this in chapter 4 of their manuals, pages 49-54.) (Suggested time: thirty minutes.)

### BEING A BRIDGE BUILDER

As a VWAP team member you are "plopped" down in a culture quite different from your own. The behaviors, values, and beliefs of the people may differ greatly from those familiar to you. With time you may come to notice the common denominators between yourself and your hosts. But the differences will hit you first. Cultural differences might be pictured in the following way. There are two cliffs: On one side is the North American way of life and on the other is the way of life found in the host country. In between looms a large chasm. In order for the two cultures to meet and understand one another, a bridge must be built connecting the two sides.

Imagine your upcoming journey as an apprenticeship in bridge building. You can lay the beam, erect a scaffolding, and forge cables that make communication between your worlds possible. Surprise your host community with your initiative at bridge building and you will find their hands joining yours.

Building the bridge involves a number of things you can think through before going, as well as others you can work on while you are there. Unfortunately, some people go on short-term teams and never work at building the bridge. They deprive themselves of some very important personal experiences, which tragically limits their understanding and curtails their growth.

Bridge building is an exciting challenge! In fact, we believe you will come to appreciate the world opening to you so much that you will continue to build bridges for the rest of your life.

### Bridge Building Involves Examining Your Stereotypes

All of us maintain certain stereotypes about other people. Some are based on elements of truth. Others grow out of myths or false perceptions. It is unfair to judge or evaluate a person based on stereotypes about the group he or she belongs to. God created individuals who are uniquely different, and should be treated as such.

Building the bridge begins with examining stereotypes: the ones you may hold and the ones the nationals may hold about you. Let's think through them.

| STEREOTYPES NORTH AMERICANS HAVE ABOUT PEOPLE IN THE THIRD WORLD | |
| --- | --- |
| NEGATIVE | POSITIVE |
| Innocent | Interdependent with family |
| Lazy | Living in harmony with life |
| Inefficient | Very spiritual |
| Slow | Content |
| Indifferent | Servant attitude |
| Corrupt | |
| Poor | |
| Uneducated | |
| Needing help | |
| Controlled by customs | |

When you arrive in the host country, you will be viewed in a certain way just because you are a North American. Doesn't seem fair, does it? But is there an element of truth in these views? Think about the stereotypes that follow, then answer the questions in the spaces provided.

| STEREOTYPES OTHERS HAVE OF NORTH AMERICANS | |
| --- | --- |
| NEGATIVE | POSITIVE |
| Aggressive | Educated |
| Harshly pragmatic | Reliable |
| Tense | Strong individuals |
| Discontent | Secured better lives |
| Lonely | Free of superstition |
| Corrupt | Confident |
| Wealthy and materialistic | Organized |
| Dominating | |
| Loud and obnoxious | |
| Overbearing | |
| Competitive | |
| Selfish/self-centered | |
| Attitude of national superiority | |
| Preoccupied with efficiency | |

**Questions for Reflection**
1. As you look through this list, what is your reaction? How do you feel?

2. Which of these apply to you? Would others see these in you?

3. Do you feel that you hold some of the stereotypes listed for people in the Third World? Which ones do you think may be valid? Why?

4. How might these stereotypes hinder the bridge-building process?

You cannot change the fact that you are a North American. And you will be perceived stereotypically from time to time. This is not all bad. Stereotypes can have some merit and facilitate understanding. But as you know from experience, not every individual embodies all the characteristics of a particular stereotype. To be a bridge builder you need to understand the reasons behind stereotypes. We bomb the bridge when we judge people without attempting to understand or allow them a chance to explain themselves.

**Bridge Building Involves Remembering Your Roles**
There are three "roles" you will play that contribute to your ability as a bridge builder.

- *The role of being a "guest" of the culture.* Think of being a guest in someone's home. How would you behave, react, interact, etc.? Or conversely, what expectations would you have of a guest in your

home? What might please and/or irritate you?
- *The role of being a "student" of the culture.* Think of yourself as a person who is there to study and learn. How does a student in school get an A? What behaviors contribute to their success?
- *The role of being a "servant" within the culture.* Think of being a person who serves everyone he or she encounters in the country. How does a servant approach those whom he or she serves? How does a servant handle differences in others?

### Bridge Building Involves the Following Applications

*Accepting:* Accept the fact that you will not completely understand the people in just one trip. This is just a beginning, so don't become too frustrated with yourself.

*Awareness:* Be aware that at times you may feel your prejudices. You may become frustrated with the way things are or the way people behave. Don't deny the feelings, own them. Only then can you begin to understand the reasons behind them. Why are you frustrated? Being aware will help you grow in understanding the differences.

*Listening:* Listen more than you talk. You are there to learn, not to instruct. The right to instruct is earned by demonstrating respect.

*Giving:* Give of yourself. Take the initiative in group settings to reach out to the nationals. People can tend to shy away from contact with nationals, especially if they aren't fluent in the language. Go ahead! Take a risk and try to speak the language. People will really appreciate the effort. And don't worry, they'll forgive you when you mess up.

*Enjoying:* Enjoy the people, their culture, and their language. If you don't take yourself too seriously, you can have more fun. Help create an environment where they can enjoy you and your culture and language just as you aim to enjoy theirs.

❖ ❖ ❖

### ◆ Personal Preparation

Have the team break into groups of three to discuss personal goals. Before leaving on the trip, make a copy of each person's goals, then follow up with each team member individually in the field.

The personal goals worksheet is a great tool to use when praying for and encouraging team members. (Team members can find this in chapter 4 of their manuals, page 53.) (Suggested time: twenty minutes.)

## PERSONAL GOALS

Thoughtfully and prayerfully respond to the following. This will help you think through and crystallize where you want to grow while on the trip. It also helps the leader(s) become aware of personal expectations and potential roadblocks to goals.

1. The following are three things I hope to learn.

2. The following are three ways I hope to grow.

3. The following are potential roadblocks to my learning and growing.

❖　❖　❖

◆ **Language**
See session 3 found in chapter 11 of this manual, page 120, and chapter 5 of the team member's manual, page 64.

◆ **Logistics**
(Suggested time: thirty minutes.)

1. Review team members' financial situations.
2. Make final plans for tool or clothing drives, if applicable.
3. Assign team medic, team mechanic, team photographer, etc. (See "Involving Your Team in Problem Solving," pages 133-134.

## ◆ Assignments

1. Fill out a "Prayer Partner" form found in forms section of this manual, page 211.
2. Complete the "Release of Liability" (form 5 on page 212 in the back of this manual). It's an unhappy thing to consider, but all travel presents some risk of injury to the participants. We strongly urge you to choose destinations with team safety in mind, and encourage your team members to use caution and good sense at all times. Nonetheless, injury may occur. Some mission agencies have found it wise to ask each participant to sign a release.

## ◆ Prayer Topic

Host community.

## SESSION FOUR—WHAT TO TAKE

> ### Goal
> In this session, the team will learn more about the host country and/or important cross-cultural issues. As in prior sessions, language and logistics are addressed. (Note: Use option 1 if a knowledgeable speaker is available. If not, use option 2. Do not attempt to squeeze both into one session.

### ◆ Option 1: Host Country
Invite a speaker who has lived in or frequently visited the country/region. Ask him or her to prepare a twenty-minute presentation and answer questions. (Suggested time: forty minutes.)

### ◆ Option 2: Cross-Cultural
Invite a missionary to address the team on subjects such as others' perceptions of North Americans, cultural sensitivity, initiating friendships, differences in value systems, etc. Ask him or her to prepare a twenty-minute presentation and answer questions. (Suggested time: forty minutes.)

### ◆ Language
See session 4 in chapter 11, page 121, of this manual and chapter 5, page 65, of the team member's manual.

### ◆ Logistics
Discuss the *packing list*. (Suggested time: thirty minutes.)

Review the packing list. Be sure to customize it for your group. For example, if you are going to a cooler climate, you'll need to revise the suggested clothing list. On numerous occasions people have ended up on a VWAP with too many of the wrong items and not enough of the right ones. Be prepared for questions on everything from the length of shorts to the type of bug repellent. If you don't have an answer, be sure to write down the question and ask your contact(s). If you use phrases such as "modest bathing suits" or "Sunday attire," we suggest you define what you mean. Otherwise, your expectations may be misunderstood. *Clarity is crucial.*

Briefly review the "Packing Tips" (found on page 111), especially the tip to pack light! (This list can be found in chapter 4, pages 54-56, of the team member's manuals.) People who have done little traveling need basic advice. If you have traveled extensively, do not assume others know what you know. Tell team members in advance if their luggage will include team items—food, medical supplies, tents, etc. Provide these items a week in advance.

```
PACKING LIST
```

**Personal Items Checklist**

- ❏ toothbrush/paste/floss
- ❏ razor/shaving cream
- ❏ sunburn remedies
- ❏ small pillow/sheets/blanket
- ❏ towels/washcloth
- ❏ deodorant (please!)
- ❏ towelette packets
- ❏ soap
- ❏ toilet paper (two rolls)
- ❏ feminine hygiene items
- ❏ insect repellent/lotion
- ❏ air mattress
- ❏ beach towel
- ❏ shampoo (avoid floral, herbal, or fruit scents)
- ❏ comb/brush
- ❏ items for contact lenses (very difficult to buy there)
- ❏ suntan lotion/sunscreen (very important near the equator)
- ❏ mosquito netting (This is optional; might be good for someone who doesn't like to put on a lot of insect repellent.)
- ❏ personal medicines (Consider vitamins, allergy tabs, caladryl lotion, aspirin, and diarrhea medicine.)
- ❏ travel clothesline
- ❏ servant's attitude
- ❏ notebook for journal/pens
- ❏ flashlight/extra batteries
- ❏ pocket knife
- ❏ Bible
- ❏ passport
- ❏ positive, flexible spirit
- ❏ personal snacks
- ❏ sunglasses
- ❏ spending money (for souvenirs, gifts, occasional meals, etc.)
- ❏ big plastic cup for work site (squeeze bottles work great)
- ❏ cheap watch (maybe to give away when you leave)
- ❏ simple gifts for school children (balloons, balls, etc.)
- ❏ leather work gloves (at least one pair, two would be best)
- ❏ camera/film/batteries (film is generally very expensive overseas)
- ❏ addresses of supporters
- ❏ photos of your family, city, and country (to show new friends and host families)

## Clothing

Think about the particular climate when packing.

*The following is applicable for work-related teams*: T-shirts, cotton socks, bandannas, and underwear are your everyday basics. Work boots (if you are on a construction team), tennis shoes, thongs, hat or sun visor, and a conservative bathing suit are other necessary items.

Men should bring a couple of pairs of work pants, knee-length shorts, and evening-type outfits. Women need to know if they are permitted to work in pants or knee-length shorts. If not, bring loose-fitting, below-the-knee cotton skirts.

Bring comfortable traveling clothes and one or two nice (not extravagant) outfits for church or a nice restaurant.

*Luggage*: We recommend each person be limited to one large travel/duffel bag and a carry-on with a change of clothes in case luggage is delayed.

Since airlines allow two bags and one carry-on per passenger, team members can take an extra suitcase each for work project supplies or other team materials.

*Special items*: Instruct the team members about changes to the packing list as well as additional items not included.

---

### PACKING TIPS

(These tips can also be found in chapter 4 of the team member's manuals, pages 58-59.)

1. *Pack light.* Chances are *you* will have to carry what *you* pack!
2. Tightly secure any items that may come open while traveling. Many a team member has had to wear clothing with the fragrant smell of Pepto Bismol or shampoo.
3. Borrow what you can. No sense in making a big investment in shoes and clothing you may only wear on this trip.
4. Break new shoes in *before* the trip . . . especially new work boots. Blisters are not a pleasant experience, and they don't make for the best of moods!
5. Take luggage you don't mind damaging. Old duffel bags are probably the best.
6. Carry one change of clothes with you if traveling by plane. Sometimes luggage gets lost and/or delayed. One of the authors failed to heed this advice and lived to regret it when luggage failed to arrive for a two-week trip to Haiti.
7. Find out if laundry facilities are available. If so, you won't have to take as much clothing.
8. Take items you won't mind leaving if you see a need. Certain items are very expensive overseas and unaffordable to the people you may be working with.
9. Leave room for souvenirs; otherwise you may be sacrificing your new Reeboks for a wooden statue.
10. Pack more than enough film and batteries. These are costly in most places and may be difficult to find in a remote locale.

---

❖   ❖   ❖

◆ **Assignment**

Ask team members to look for examples of servanthood in people at work, in their homes, or in the news during this next week. Have them review the selection entitled "Being a Servant" found in session 5, page 113 of this book, and in session 5 of the team member's manual, page 57.

◆ **Prayer Topic**

The needs of the missionaries the team will work with.

---

## SESSION FIVE—BE SERVANTS

---

> **Goal**
> In this session, we will take a field trip to build relationships and/or understand more about our own culture. We will also focus on developing the attitude of a servant. (Note: Choose between option 1 and option 2, depending on which is more feasible for your group.)

◆ **Option 1: Team Dynamics**

Take a field trip such as that described below. Reconvene and discuss findings. (Suggested time: sixty minutes.)

> Rich Hurst has used a field trip to build team relations with the VWAP teams from University Presbyterian Church in Seattle. The church is near downtown, close to a street that is a popular hangout for the homeless, runaways, "punks," and other teens in trouble. Many American and foreign students attending the nearby university populate the area.
>
> Rich divides the team into groups of two to four members and gives each one an assignment. To one he may assign the task of sharing, to another, caring. He may ask another to find the directions to the nearest hospital without using any English. He is careful not to give any specifics in order to allow each group to experience the group process and problem solving. The teams head out hesitantly into the night, unsure exactly of what they should do.
>
> Forty-five minutes later they're usually back, buzzing among themselves about their little adventure. One group assigned to care reported that they found a shopkeeper still at work and borrowed his broom. They excitedly reported about their conversations with the curious street people who watched them cleaning the sidewalks. The groups usually have something positive to report and come away from the exercise with a closer bond to teammates and an increased awareness of the needs close to home.

◆ **Option 2: Team Dynamics**

Conduct a field trip to a shopping mall such as the one described below. Reconvene either at the regular meeting room or at a location in or near the mall to discuss your findings. (Suggested time: sixty minutes.)

> Doug and Jackie Millham, founders of a short-term mission training program called Discover the World, use a trip to the mall to help their groups get a better idea of North American values and how we are perceived by others. Each team member heads off to the mall with instructions to study where our society places its values. What

does the selection of shops say about how we view young people? Old people? Fat or thin people? White people or people of color? How many shops sell items that are necessary for human survival? How many sell luxury goods? Is a shopping mall reflective of the society at large? Why, or why not?

Think of your own list of questions, then head out for an evening at the mall to see it through the eyes of a stranger.[1]

### ◆ Personal Preparation
Review the "Being a Servant" exercise and discuss findings from last week's assignment. (This information can be found in the team member's manual, chapter 4, page 57.) (Suggested time: twenty minutes.)

## BEING A SERVANT

Developing and maintaining a servant's attitude do not come easily or naturally for many of us. Being a servant is something you will understand a great deal better after the trip is over. Each of us needs to encourage one another in servanthood.

*Toward Nationals:* What does it mean to be a servant to the people of the community and local church? How might this be tested? What attitudes may hinder you from being a servant to the nationals?

*Toward the Team Leader:* Team leaders have the same needs and struggles that members have. Leaders do their best to make the experience a positive and productive one for everyone. Team leaders really benefit from team members who are willing to seek ways to be a servant to them.

*Toward Fellow Team Members:* Being a servant toward one another really sums up the whole idea of being a team. Read John 13:1-17 and think through the implications of Jesus washing the disciples' feet. What does that mean for your attitude and relationship with your fellow team members?

### For Reflection
*Helper or Servant?* The dictionary defines to *help* as "to aid, assist or contribute strength; to save or rescue." *Serve* is defined as "to act as the servant of another." What do you see as the difference? What do these definitions say about those who are the objects of your help? What do they say about the objects of your service?

❖　❖　❖

### ◆ Language
See session 5 found in chapter 11, page 123, of this manual and chapter 5 of the team member's manual, page 67.

### ◆ Logistics
Review team member finances. Discuss the importance of journaling. (Suggested time: thirty minutes.)

◆ **Assignment**
Write thank-you notes to donors.

◆ **Prayer Topic**
The sending church.

## SESSION SIX—FINALIZING DETAILS

> **Goal**
> In this session, all details surrounding the actual travel will be finalized and preparations for the team's project completed.

### ◆ Miscellaneous
Tie up all the loose ends related to your specific project. For instance, if you are conducting a vacation Bible school in the host community, invite Sunday school teachers to work with the team in planning activities and games that can be executed with minimal language skills. (Suggested time: sixty minutes.)

### ◆ Language
See session 6 found in chapter 11, page 125, of this manual, and chapter 5 of the team member's manual, page 67.

### ◆ Logistics
Review all final details including when and where to meet for the flight. Distribute emergency contact telephone numbers. Make sure all team members have been inoculated and have all their travel documentation. Discuss any other last minute information, and the suggestions below. (Team members can refer to chapter 4, pages 58-59, in their manuals.) (Suggested time: forty-five minutes.)

### TRAVEL TIPS

Keep the following in mind while preparing for your trip. Before you leave, consider where you will be, who you will meet, and what you will do. Plan ahead.

1. Photocopy your passport and give the copy to the team leader for use in case of emergency.
2. Some of the people you meet will enjoy seeing pictures of your family and hometown. Be sure to take a few snapshots and postcards to show them. (Be sensitive of your audience's feelings; your relative affluence may offend some people.)
3. Remember to pack lightly. You will be glad you did!
4. Remember that your dress code will be dictated by the host culture, not your own tastes. Consider leaving all your jewelry behind; this prevents theft as well as the possibility of offending others.
5. Bring small, inexpensive gifts to share with your hosts.
6. Leave your hair dryer at home! Often electrical currents and contact pins are different abroad.

7. Leave a complete itinerary with a friend or family member.
8. Make sure the team leader and your church office have the name, address, and phone number of a contact person for you.
9. Check your wallet and remove anything that won't be needed on the trip. Beware of potential pickpockets while traveling in large cities.
10. Stick with other team members while traveling to avoid being left behind or separated from the group.
11. Write down the flight information if traveling by air in case you do become separated.
12. Upon arrival, hold *all* your bags tightly while in the crowded and confusing airport.
13. Listen well to the team leader once you arrive at the airport and follow his or her instructions quickly.
14. If traveling by airplane, be aware of the image you are projecting to those around you. Be sensitive to the nationals from your host country who are on board the flight.
15. In many areas, septic systems are not designed to handle toilet paper. If there is a waste receptacle next to the toilet, this is generally a clue that toilet paper is meant to be thrown away, not flushed.
16. If you suffer from any kind of travel sickness, bring proper medication. Remember, it may be difficult for the team to slow down or stop for you to recuperate. Taking these precautions is both helpful and thoughtful.

❖   ❖   ❖

◆ **Prayer Topic**
Travel.

---

NOTE     1. Adapted from Jacquelyn D. Millham, *Discover the World, Leader's Guide* (Pasadena, CA: Discover the World, Inc., 1990), pages 61-62.

# CHAPTER ELEVEN

# LANGUAGE LEARNING

Learning a foreign language. For some, it's an exciting adventure: making strange sounds that somehow have meaning to others, listening for words related to familiar English words, feeling the thrill of understanding someone for the first time. For others, it's a nightmare: incomprehensible sounds coming at a thousand per second, the frustration of not being able to express even the most simple sentiment, the mental block that embarrassment produces.

Well, this course is for everyone! The six sessions on the following pages are adapted from a course that has successfully calmed the fears of those nervous around foreign language and encouraged those who love tackling new languages.

It includes almost everything you need for teaching the language. All you add is the teacher! It's up to you to locate someone with skill in the language the team needs to learn and the enthusiasm to make the class a fun and rewarding experience for all students. (These sessions are found in chapter 5 of the team member's manual, beginning on page 60.)

## POINTERS FOR THE INSTRUCTOR

1. Don't try to teach too much material. The information in this chapter is enough without being overwhelming. Encourage students to use proper pronunciation and feel confident with just a few phrases. The late Dr. Tom Brewster of Fuller Seminary encouraged his students to "learn a little, use it a lot!"[1]
2. Don't let one or two students dominate the class. The others will become frustrated and may stop trying to figure things out for themselves.
3. There is a proper etiquette for speaking English with people who have very little English ability. Remind students to speak slowly and clearly, that speaking louder will not help, and to use common words—if the listener seems confused, think of an alternative word.
4. Be silly and creative. Try to create an energetic but nonthreatening environment for the students. If someone does especially well, paste a big gold star on his or her forehead! Keep the atmosphere lighthearted.

## SESSION ONE

---

**Goal**
Get the class accustomed to hearing and making new sounds.

---

◆ **Exercise One**
The alphabet. Explain that letters in the other language are not pronounced the same as they are in English. Show the class how each letter is pronounced, including letters that are not in the English alphabet (in Spanish, the letters ch, ll, rr, for example). Going around the room, have each student practice pronouncing one letter of the alphabet until all letters have been pronounced. Be patient with students who are having trouble but work toward very accurate pronunciation.

◆ **Exercise Two**
Learning names. Write the foreign language equivalent of each student's name on the board. Each student attempts to correctly pronounce his or her name. Repeat until all students have been taught the new pronunciation of their name.

◆ **Exercise Three**
Song. Teach a simple Christian chorus that has the same tune as one sung in English. The best song to use for Spanish is "Allelu" because of its simplicity and body movements. (Lyrics to the three Spanish-language choruses mentioned in this section are found on pages 126-127 in this chapter; page 70 of team member's manual.)

## SESSION TWO

> **Goal**
> Show the class that they probably know more of the foreign language than they think.

### ◆ Exercise One
Review the alphabet by pronouncing it several times as a group. Then go around the room, one letter at a time.

### ◆ Exercise Two
Introductions. Teach class how to say, "Hello, my name is _____," using the names they learned last week. Have each team member introduce himself or herself to the others.

### ◆ Exercise Three
John 3:16. Hand the class the words to John 3:16 in the foreign language, but don't tell them what it is. Going around the room, have each person pronounce the words, one word to a person, until the verse is complete. Have them guess what it is by pointing out the words that are similar to English. For example, in Spanish, *único* (only) is like the English word *unique*; *cree* (believes) is like the English word *creed*. (Note: Encourage those who have a fair knowledge of the language to hold back so that others can have fun figuring things out for themselves.)

### ◆ Exercise Four
Vocabulary. Begin teaching basic vocabulary related to Scripture and church life.

| ENGLISH | SPANISH | OTHER |
|---|---|---|
| God | Dios | |
| Jesus | Jesús | |
| Jesus Christ | Jesucristo | |
| the Lord | el Señor | |
| Protestant | evangélico(a) | |
| Catholic | Católico(a) | |
| the Holy Bible | la Santa Biblia | |
| Matthew | San Mateo | |
| Mark | San Marcos | |
| Luke | San Lucas | |
| John | San Juan | |
| Acts | Los Hechos | |
| Praise God! | ¡Gloria a Dios! | |
| we pray | oramos | |
| to love | amar | |

## SESSION THREE

> **Goal**
> Begin to build a vocabulary and get a very basic understanding of the grammar.

### ◆ Exercise One
Review. Practice John 3:16 and last week's vocabulary.

### ◆ Exercise Two
Numbers. Teach numbers from one to twenty, plus multiples of ten up to one hundred. Going around the room, have the group count to fifty, one person to a number.

| NUMBERS | |
|---|---|
| 1 _____ | 15 _____ |
| 2 _____ | 16 _____ |
| 3 _____ | 17 _____ |
| 4 _____ | 18 _____ |
| 5 _____ | 19 _____ |
| 6 _____ | 20 _____ |
| 7 _____ | 30 _____ |
| 8 _____ | 40 _____ |
| 9 _____ | 50 _____ |
| 10 _____ | 60 _____ |
| 11 _____ | 70 _____ |
| 12 _____ | 80 _____ |
| 13 _____ | 90 _____ |
| 14 _____ | 100 _____ |

### ◆ Exercise Three
Grammar. Keeping in mind that grammar is horrifying to some, boring to most, and of interest to only a few, offer a very brief overview of how verbs are conjugated. Help students to understand how verb endings will often agree with pronouns in identifying who is acting out the verb (Romance languages). Show them that once they know any one verb they will be able to recognize all other words related to it. (With Spanish, use a very basic, regular verb like *amar*. Discuss only present tense.)

### ◆ Exercise Four
Song. Teach a simple chorus that uses a conjugated verb so that students can see the grammar lesson applied. For Spanish, the song "I Love You Lord (and I lift my voice)" is good because it uses an infinitive verb (*adorar*), a direct object pronoun (*te amo*), and a simple conjugation (*levanto*).

## SESSION FOUR

**Goal**
Be able to introduce oneself and give a brief personal description.

◆ **Exercise One**
Review. Go over numbers again, concentrating on pronunciation.

◆ **Exercise Two**
More vocabulary. Teach the class words they can use to say something about themselves.

My name is _____.

I have a _____.

| | | | |
|---|---|---|---|
| Brother | _____ | Sister | _____ |
| Husband | _____ | Wife | _____ |
| Child | _____ | Grandchild | _____ |

I am a _____.

| | | | |
|---|---|---|---|
| Brother | _____ | Sister | _____ |
| Husband | _____ | Wife | _____ |
| Grandfather | _____ | Grandmother | _____ |

My job is a _____.

| | | | |
|---|---|---|---|
| Teacher | _____ | Engineer | _____ |
| Farmer | _____ | Pastor | _____ |
| Office worker | _____ | Other | _____ |

The word for my occupation is _____.

I live in the United States _____ Canada _____.

I like _____.

| | | | |
|---|---|---|---|
| Skiing | _____ | Animals | _____ |
| Books | _____ | Sports | _____ |
| Music | _____ | Other | _____ |

Teach each person how to say the necessary words to complete this exercise.

◆ **Exercise Three**
Still more vocabulary. Teach the students the names of ten common foods
they are likely to encounter.

|  | FOREIGN WORD | SPELLED PHONETICALLY | ENGLISH EQUIVALENT |
|---|---|---|---|
| 1. | _____ | _____ | _____ |
| 2. | _____ | _____ | _____ |
| 3. | _____ | _____ | _____ |
| 4. | _____ | _____ | _____ |
| 5. | _____ | _____ | _____ |
| 6. | _____ | _____ | _____ |
| 7. | _____ | _____ | _____ |
| 8. | _____ | _____ | _____ |
| 9. | _____ | _____ | _____ |
| 10. | _____ | _____ | _____ |

◆ **Exercise Four**
In groups of three, have the students help one another think of a five-
sentence personal description. You should participate. After a few minutes
preparation, bring the group back together and have each person stand to
say his five sentences.

◆ **Exercise Five**
Songs. Sing both songs that the class has learned.

## SESSION FIVE

**Goal**
Be able to ask others about themselves.

◆ **Exercise One**
Review. Go over all vocabulary to this point, concentrating on last week's.

◆ **Exercise Two**
New words. Teach students the translations of the following phrases. After they're comfortable with the material, have one person (A) ask another (B) a question. When B has answered A, have B turn to another person (C) and ask a question. Continue until all team members have answered and asked a question.

---

QUESTIONS FOR CHILDREN

Hello! What's your name?

How old are you?

Do you have brothers and sisters?

What grade are you in?

---

QUESTIONS FOR ADULTS

Hello! What is your name?

Where do you work?

Where do you live?

What foods do you like?

| QUESTIONS FOR PARENTS |
|---|
| How many children do you have? |
| How old are they? |
| What is this boy's name? |
| Does he like school? |
| What does he like? |

◆ **Exercise Three**

Song. Teach another simple chorus. For Spanish, the song "Ho, Ho, Ho, Hosannah" is a fun one to teach (page 126).

## SESSION SIX

> **Goal**
> Give the student confidence that he or she now knows at least a few phrases that can be used in many situations.

◆ **Exercise One**
Review pronunciation. Have each student look up his or her favorite verse in a Bible printed in the foreign language. As he or she reads it aloud, other students should try to guess which verse it is.

◆ **Exercise Two**
Vocabulary. Teach the survival phrases listed here.

> Please.
>
> Thank you.
>
> Please speak more slowly.
>
> One moment, please.
>
> I don't speak much (name of language).
>
> Do you speak English?
>
> I'm lost. Where is the (church, mission, etc.)?
>
> I need a doctor.
>
> I'm sorry.
>
> God bless you!
>
> Very good!
>
> I'm tired.
>
> I don't feel well.
>
> Where is the bathroom?

◆ **Exercise Three**
Songs. Review all three songs.

## SONGS FOR TEAMS LEARNING SPANISH

In churches where the congregation worships in Spanish, you may hear many songs composed in the local style of music. However, you may also hear some familiar tunes that have been "imported" at some time in the past and translated. The songs below are three such songs you can learn and join the congregation in singing. (See page 70 in team member's manual.)

### Allelu

| | |
|---|---|
| Allelu, Allelu, Allelu, Allelujah | Alelu, Alelu, Alelu, Alelúia |
| **Praise ye the Lord!** | **Gloria al Señor!** |
| Allelu, Allelu, Allelu, Allelujah | Alelu, Alelu, Alelu, Alelúia |
| **Praise ye the Lord!** | **Gloria al Señor!** |
| | |
| **Praise ye the Lord!** | **Gloria al Señor!** |
| Allelujah! | Alelúia! |
| **Praise ye the Lord!** | **Gloria al Señor!** |
| Allelujah! | Alelúia! |
| **Praise ye the Lord!** | **Gloria al Señor!** |
| Allelujah! | Alelúia! |
| *Praise ye the Lord!* | *Gloria al Señor!* |

Women stand to sing the first line, then sit. Men stand to sing the second line (bold) then sit. Continue through song, standing each time it's your turn to sing. All stand and sing the final line (italics).

### I Love You Lord

| | |
|---|---|
| I love You Lord | Te amo Rey |
| and I lift my voice, | y levanto mi voz, |
| to worship You. | para adorar. |
| Oh my soul rejoice! | y gozarme en ti! |
| | |
| Take joy my King | Regocíjate, |
| in what You hear. | escucha mi Rey. |
| Let it be a sweet, | Que sea un dulce |
| sweet sound in Your ear. | sonar para tí. |

### Ho, Ho, Ho, Hosannah

| | |
|---|---|
| Ho, ho, ho, hosannah | Jo, jo, jo, josanah |
| Ha, ha, hallelujah | Ja, ja, jaleluia |
| He, He, He died for me | He, He, He, el murió por mi |
| I've got the joy of the Lord! | ¡Yo le alabaré! |

(Remember, the letter J in Spanish is pronounced like an English H. The H in Spanish is silent. So "he, he, el" sounds like "eh, eh, el.")

---

NOTE    1. From the videotape *Building Cross-Cultural Relationships* by Dr. E. Thomas Brewster (Pasadena, CA: Institute of Biblical Studies, 1983).

CHAPTER TWELVE

# EXPECTING
# THE UNEXPECTED

No matter how well you plan, how many weeks of training classes you have with the team, and how many long-distance phone calls you place to the on-field host, something unexpected is going to happen! As a leader you need to expect the unexpected. The word you will emphasize over and over again with your team is *flexibility*. Make sure it's a word you're familiar with as well. When traveling overseas one invariably encounters the unexpected. The following are some unexpected or unplanned things that have happened to us (or others) while on teams. It could happen to you!

## SICK TEAM MEMBER(S)

There will undoubtedly be a bit of sickness on any VWAP team, so don't become immediately alarmed. Some good health guidelines are given in chapter 10, page 101, such as, "Don't hesitate to seek medical attention." Colds often spread quickly on teams, and with the change in diet and climate there are usually touches of diarrhea. The thing to watch for is dehydration. If a person's condition seems to deteriorate, you may have to consider sending him or her home—you can't afford any "heroic" attitudes. This, of course, is a last resort, but not beyond consideration. One further suggestion: Isolate team members who have contagious illnesses to prevent them from spreading. (See the suggested medical kit, page 102.)

## DISRUPTIVE TEAM MEMBERS
## (ISSUES OF POWER AND CONTROL)

Sally led a team that worked with a ministry that was constructing homes for poor families. Due to a number of circumstances, she had not been able to fill all the openings. When Jerry expressed an interest in participating, Sally added him to the team, even though he had missed valuable class time.

From the outset, Jerry began to make it clear that he had his own agenda for the VWAP. The host ministry had asked the team to help with housing construction; he intended to teach first-aid classes. The hosts invited the team to sit with the congregation during church; he intended to lead music. When the team went to a beach community for R & R, Jerry complained the hotel was too far from the beach and set out to find a new one. Since nonrefundable deposits had been paid on lodging and van rental, Sally made the decision that the team would not transfer to a new hotel. For the next three days, Jerry never missed an opportunity to grumble about the "poor" choice of a hotel.

We hope that you'll be able to root out this type of problem during the interview and training phases of the VWAP, but nevertheless, a complainer, or "well-intentioned dragon" (to use Marshall Shelley's phrase), may slip through. A disruptive team member can be a detriment not only to the team but to the work of the local missionary and/or national church as well. The situation should be dealt with promptly.

Each team member must understand that the sending church has entrusted the leadership of the team with the control and direction of the team. This is not negotiable. If that person does not like the way things are, then he or she may have to be sent home. Let the person know there will be a time to discuss his or her concerns with the proper church leadership, but the on-field portion of the VWAP is not the time or place. Leaders need to remember their responsibility is to lead the team, not to run a popularity contest.

In some cases the "problem" that is troubling the team member may not be the real issue. Sitting down with the person and allowing him or her to talk it out may resolve the difficulty. Let the person know you care about him or her. Be familiar with the person's reason for being there as this will help you understand his or her expectations and frustrations.

## DEALING WITH COUPLES

Whether your team is composed of married couples, singles, or a mixture, the "couple issue" is going to arise. Married or dating couples can both benefit from and contribute to the community of the team. In all cases though, some ground rules need to be made clear. The following are questions for you to address with couples:

1. *Do you understand that the trip is not a time to work on problems in the relationship?* Emotional energy is drained from the whole team when a couple becomes preoccupied with working out their differences. Regardless of the circumstances, the VWAP is not the time to "break up" or to test each other's devotion.
2. *Are you clear that the VWAP is about investing emotionally in other team members and members of the host community?* If you become preoccupied with one another, you cannot effectively bond with others.
3. *Will you be able to talk freely with the leader(s) if your relationship becomes an issue?*
4. *Do you see the artificial nature of the VWAP environment?* In this situation, a couple's relationship is subject to a fishbowl of scrutiny. Can you

be natural under these conditions, or will one party tend to withdraw? Team living also offers more built-in supports, which can make a couple feel like they need each other less. They must recognize that this sort of support is not duplicated back home.

Often the excitement, adventure, and indeed romance of a VWAP experience causes some team members to become attracted to one another. Before the trip begins, encourage team members to consider the following:

- Any relationship that is "destined to be" can wait ten to fifteen days until you get home! Your budding romance may cause you to become emotionally isolated from your teammates and the host community.
- The emotional strain of some VWAP experiences may cause a need for dependence that evaporates upon returning home. Don't confuse romantic interest with what may simply be genuine emotional support, offered by a team member in this unique environment.

## MISUNDERSTANDINGS WITH THE HOSTS IN THE COUNTRY

Communication is the key to a successful VWAP. The more teams you lead, the more you will appreciate this fact. Poor communication can elicit misunderstandings between your team and the hosts in the country. One team leader experienced confusion about the use of the host's vehicle in the field. He had understood that the host would loan his vehicle for transport to and from the worksite. However, when the team arrived, he learned the host had no intention of letting the team use the vehicle. Consequently, they ended up walking a lot!

Misunderstandings often arise over expectations regarding work, transportation, money, ministries, number of people, lodging, etc. When this occurs, rather than blaming your host, sit down for an honest heart-to-heart talk with him or her. You both want to accomplish the same things, so discuss how you may be able to work together to this end. Agree to resolve the communication difficulties once you are home. Remember, the on-field portion of the VWAP is not the place to figure out what went wrong.

## STALLED/DELAYED WORK OR MINISTRY PROJECT

In 1987, a team set out for a school-building project in Haiti. Upon arrival, a national strike was called to protest the existing regime. The team was unable to travel to and from the work-site while the strike was in process. Therefore, they had to spend several days waiting at the guest house in which they were staying. Traveling in Third-World countries quickly teaches you that things are not always predictable. We have experienced delays with projects on numerous occasions. The reasons vary but have included restrictive weather (rains, hurricanes, etc.), political turmoil, and supply delays.

A team faces several choices when this happens. They can grumble and complain, or they can accept the circumstances. We suggest that as the leader you encourage them to make do. Utilize the delays for relationship development with nationals, missionaries, and other team members. Spend extended time in prayer for the situation and the attitudes with which the people are struggling. Along with prayer, spend extended time in group study and discussion related to world involvement. *Be creative with the unexpected "free" time you have been given!*

## TRANSPORTATION DIFFICULTIES

If you are using a church, mission agency, or rented van, count on it breaking down. Remember, *flexibility!*

Transportation difficulties can and often do cause a great deal of stress for the team. Anticipate the difficulties of traveling in a Third-World country. And count yourself very, very fortunate if there are no debacles!

Transportation difficulties may require you to come up with quick alternatives. It will help if you have someone well-versed in the language and local customs assisting you, because he or she will be able to get things done more quickly. Explain to the team that waiting is part of the cultural experience. In fact, the longer the wait, the greater the experience!

One thing to keep in mind is that you may find yourself getting more frustrated and stressed out than the team as a whole. This is because you feel the pressure of schedule. When this occurs, ease up a bit and go with the flow. Remember, God is as interested in remaking you as He is interested in making the project. Let the team see that you can trust God to handle difficulties.

## ANXIOUS RELATIVES

Anxious relatives start surfacing about the time the idea of going first enters a team member's head. The relative first attempts to nonchalantly brush off the idea. When the team member begins putting down money and buying books on the country, the strategy changes. The relative suddenly becomes an expert on a country he or she once barely knew existed. Negative news stories published in any English-speaking newspaper begin turning up in the team member's mailbox or on his or her doorstep. Then the relative starts calling with horror stories from friends who once knew someone who knew someone who met someone who used to visit there and had a bad experience! When this fails, the relative pulls out the big guns: "If you really loved me. . . ."

This scenario sounds farfetched, but it is the actual experience of one thirty-five-year-old traveler. For many team members, the person described above could be their own father, or sister, or spouse.

People who are concerned for the health and safety of a team member may be made extremely anxious by their loved one's upcoming trip. Remember not to make light of these concerns. The best way to handle a relative's concern is to have the team member provide the most detailed information possible, including emergency numbers where the team can be reached. Have the member call home at least once if possible, assuring the person he or she is safe. In all cases, the team member should phone home as soon as the team returns. Most of the assurances will have to come from the team members themselves, but as a leader, be prepared to ease some fears yourself.

## UNFORESEEN CIRCUMSTANCES

### Lost Money
When traveling with large sums of cash, do not keep it in your back pocket or in your purse. Strap it discreetly to you, using a money belt or hidden pouch. When possible, use traveler's checks and/or credit cards. Do not be obvious with your money. It is an invitation to a potential pickpocket. Keep the cash (and passports) in a hotel or office safe, if possible. But in any case, be sure it is secure. Your host should be able to assist you here.

If you need to lay out a large sum for the hotel at the R & R spot, make sure you carry traveler's checks. When carrying amounts larger than $500, have someone else on the team carry half of the traveler's checks. Since you'll need the receipt to replace any lost or stolen checks, you should each carry the receipts that correspond to the other person's group of checks. Inquire as to what things may be paid for with a church check.

### Lost Luggage
If a team member loses luggage, all you can do is continue to pester the airline that lost it. It is *very* important for the leader to hold on to the claim numbers. These numbers are crucial for locating lost baggage! Remind team members to carry a change of clothing with them on the plane.

### Accidents/Deaths
When accidents happen, act quickly. In fact, we suggest having a contingency plan worked out with the host in case of an accident or a death. In either case, contact your immediate leader at your sending church to get input. In the case of a death, the team leader should defer to the missionary's or host's knowledge of local legal requirements.

## INVOLVING YOUR TEAM IN PROBLEM SOLVING

With the help of your team, small problems need not become big ones. Assign each team member partial responsibility for your contingency plans. For example, the team mechanic should bring tools and the necessary knowhow to perform emergency roadside repairs on the team's bus or vans. A little advance planning can save hours of aggravation and delay. The team medic should know the basics of first aid and be ready to handle minor medical emergencies.

Aside from getting the team out of a jam, the team medic and mechanic get the chance to be responsible for a small part of the trip. Why not try to make each person "special" by assigning each one a job. Some of the job titles might be team photographer, videographer, accountant, food organizer, navigator, construction foreman, translator, and team pastor. Be creative. Try to find a way to use each person's gifts for a special role on your trip.

## THE THREE-CRISIS RULE

The team leader, as well as the team members, would do well to keep the three-crisis rule in mind for all foreign travel and large group activities. The rule is simply this: Assume that three things will go wrong no matter how well you plan. Adopt the attitude that contingencies will arise. Who knows what they will be? Someone may become ill, the bus may break down, or the rooms at the hotel may have been given away.

When you begin the trip with this attitude, you are preparing to be flexible as well as facing the fact that you cannot always be in control or trust in your own strength. Encourage one another to practice the mental attitude of accepting both the major and minor changes in plans that inevitably occur with foreign travel. If nothing goes "wrong" with your team, fine . . . but you will have missed some rewarding opportunities to see the Lord work. Difficulties give you the opportunity to discover your inner resolve. And in the face of adversity, the team can be surprised by the hidden strengths and talents that emerge in some.

# PART FOUR
# ON THE FIELD

*For several months, your energy has been focused on reaching this point. Soon, you and the team will be departing on your Vacation with a Purpose. While this is probably the most exciting stage in the VWAP, it is also the time when things become most hectic and confusing for the leader. The next section will provide the information you need to feel comfortable with the responsibility of leading a team through the rigors of travel. We hope the suggestions will help you deal with the circumstances you will confront in unfamiliar surroundings.*

*This part of the book deals extensively with international travel. Nonetheless, teams staying within their own countries will find much of the information to be useful.*

CHAPTER THIRTEEN

# TRAVEL DETAILS

Believe it or not, traveling with a team may be the toughest part of Vacations with a Purpose. Granted, you're working with adults, but there is something about traveling that can cause people to become childlike and confused at times. Don't believe it?

- On one of our trips, several team members spent all the time before the flight at the wrong airport gate. It finally dawned on them that there were no other people from their team with them, so they began to search for the rest of us. We finally met somewhere in the middle, with very little time to spare!
- On another occasion, the team had met at the ticket counter to check their bags. After everything was checked in, the team leader handed out the tickets and instructed them to walk, as a group, to the departure gate and board the airplane. For some reason (which is still a mystery to me!), two team members decided to stop and have a cup of coffee at the airport cafeteria. Unfortunately, their absence wasn't noticed until mid-flight! They eventually rejoined the team at their destination, but their little coffee break caused the team six hours of travel delay.

Since the actual travel days present your greatest logistical challenges, we have prepared two checklists for you to refer to. They'll assist you before and during your travel to the host city, and once you arrive. The less time you spend worrying, the more you can enjoy the company of the team members.

## TRAVEL DAY CHECKLIST

❏ Confirm flight times and reservations at least twenty-four hours in advance.

❏ Make sure each team member knows exactly where and when to meet. If the team is meeting at the airport, have them meet two hours before flight time. Stress promptness!

❏ Do not have individual team members check in for flight; check in as a group. The team is traveling as a group and the airline requires groups to check in together.

❏ Do not give plane tickets to team members until it's time to board the airplane. Collect the return tickets soon after boarding. This avoids the possibility of someone misplacing his or her ticket and creating time delays for the entire group.

❏ Identify the team's luggage with a bright, highly visible tag of some kind. Keep all baggage claim checks together. (In some groups, the leader passes out colored ribbon or fluorescent tape at the airport, which team members attach to their bags prior to check-in.)

❏ Assign a "buddy" to each person on the team. Buddies are responsible to know, at all times, where the other is. When a team member takes a walk or runs to the market, that team member must inform his or her buddy. If both buddies separate from the group, it's their responsibility to tell someone where they will be.

❏ Have all necessary cash and/or checks you will need for the trip.

❏ Have your own passport and any other necessary identification.

❏ Make sure each team member has his or her passport and any other necessary identification.

❏ Have the phone number of the contact in the host country in case he or she is not at the airport, or in case of delays. If possible, have a backup phone number of a secondary contact.

❏ Leave emergency numbers for each team member with someone in the church office.

❏ Have a copy of all previous correspondence with overseas contact or host (in case of misunderstandings).

❏ Have one extra copy of team member's manual in case someone forgets or loses his or hers.

❏ Review the travel tips found in chapter 10, pages 115-116 (session 6, pages 58-59, of team member's manual), with your team at a meeting and on the actual day of departure.

## ON-FIELD ARRIVAL TIPS

On-field arrival is an event. As team members file off the plane into an unfamiliar airport, the pace of events increases immensely. It will be helpful for you to read through this list of tips prior to the trip and then review them again while on the plane. We hope by doing so you can avoid losing baggage or, worse yet, a team member at the airport!

1. Help team members fill out the tourist cards correctly. We suggest doing yours as a sample and passing it around. Collect tourist cards and passports from team members immediately after they clear customs, unless you're going to a country where it is advisable for team members to carry theirs at all times. Check ahead with your hosts regarding this.
2. Encourage the team to stick together once they leave the plane. The airport scene may very well be congested and crazy. And someone could inadvertently get separated from the group.
3. Go through immigration last in case a team member has a problem. (Once a passenger clears the customs area, he or she is not allowed to reenter.)
4. As luggage is claimed keep it all in one stack. Be sure all members have their luggage *before* anyone goes through customs.
5. If a bag is missing, report it immediately to the proper authorities.
6. Instruct team members to wait outside customs doors for you. If there are two or more leaders, have one go first and one go last through customs.
7. Emphasize that team members should hold their bags tightly and not let anyone help them.
8. Have some small bills in your pocket in case there is a need for tipping.
9. Once contact is made with the host, load the team quickly into the vehicle. (The team will not usually move very fast, so you may have to gently push them!)
10. The less said during immigration and customs, the better.

## ON-FIELD FINANCIAL RECORDKEEPING

Keeping track of the finances for the team is important, not only for your VWAP, but for the planning of future teams. It is easy, with all the events you will have on your trip, to let this area slip. The sheet and instructions given here are intended to facilitate accurate and consistent recordkeeping.

Form 3 in the back of this book (page 210) is an accounting form for keeping track of the money while on your trip. Complete three copies of the form as follows:

1. Before your departure, review this procedure with your church finance office and discuss any additional instructions they may have regarding accounting procedures.

2. Record the expenditure in its proper column, and include the date and purpose of the expense.

3. When one sheet is full, total the columns at the bottom and put the sum of all totals in the upper-left corner in the space marked "total amount spent." Do the same for all sheets.

4. On the final sheet, total the sums of all previous sheets and write the grand total in the upper-left corner. Sign all sheets and complete the top portion.

5. Photocopy the sheets upon return and submit them, along with any left-over funds, to the church finance office.

# CHAPTER FOURTEEN

# PERSONAL
# AND SPIRITUAL GROWTH

"Dave walked over to his bookshelf and scanned the titles. Hidden among the novels and old college textbooks was the thin, red volume, the only book that had no title printed on the spine. He pulled the book from the shelf and sat down to read the words he had penned four years earlier.

*What I was thinking back then?* thought Dave as he began leafing through the pages of his journal. He was to speak to a Sunday school class about his experiences on a Vacation with a Purpose. His journal seemed the best place to begin his preparation.

As he read the pages, he became aware of two emerging patterns. First, his journal entries became more introspective as the trip progressed. Early entries noted the sights, sounds, and interactions that so overwhelmed him. The latter entries focused less on externals, and more on what Dave was feeling and learning through his experience.

Second, the journal seemed to be written by a stranger. The tone of the entries was timid, unsure, apprehensive. Dave chuckled, remembering his relief at finding that the mission station needed carpentry skills. He could work in complete solitude, free from any interaction with missionaries, church members, or fellow teammates.

Dave realized that in the few years since the trip he had developed a new confidence. Now he was a lay leader in the church, partially responsible for one of the large fellowship groups. On Sunday he would be ordained as a deacon, a position requiring a lot of personal interaction, often with people he'd never met. He smiled when he realized that many people assumed he had always possessed his ability to talk freely with others and encourage them in their struggles. The pages of his journal offered plenty of evidence to the contrary.

The entry written on day eleven seemed to Dave to hold a clue to the transformation that had occurred in him during the last several years. He had written about discovering that God could use "even him" to touch others, just as God was using the men, women, and children of the village to touch him. Furthermore, he was learning that the best way to make yourself useful to God "is to be obedient—not necessarily well-schooled, or super-religious—just obedient and available."

*It's funny,* thought Dave, *that I had to go so many miles, spend twelve days eating lousy food, and work so hard, to learn something as elementary as what God wants from me.* **99**

❖   ❖   ❖

Dave is like countless other team members who have grown personally and spiritually as a result of their participation in a Vacation with a Purpose. In Dave's case, the results were greater self-confidence and the awareness that he has what it takes to be someone God can use. For others, the discoveries may differ but the potential for growth is the same.

One of your major responsibilities while on the field is to encourage the personal and spiritual growth of the team members. As a leader, you cannot force people to grow, but you can create an environment where growth is encouraged.

Team pastor Dick Pyle made his teammates' spiritual growth a high priority on his Vacation with a Purpose. He prepared a series of talks based on the Psalms, which helped the team draw parallels between the daily experiences of their VWAP and their lives in Christ. During the trip he met with each team member, questioning and encouraging them to probe the broader application of the lessons they were learning.

Make it a point to try to talk one-on-one with each team member every day. In the natural course of daily activity, initiate a conversation about what they are learning, thinking, and/or feeling. Avoid the natural tendency to talk only with those whose company you enjoy and appreciate.

Remind the team periodically throughout the trip of the value of journaling and personal devotions. Like Dave, team members will appreciate having a record of their thoughts. The best exhortation will be your own example. Be sure to model what you are teaching.

There are pages in the team member manual that give them a place to record events, thoughts, and reflections. These journaling pages are duplicated in this book as appendix A, pages 186-199. No matter how many trips like this you have led, be sure you take some time out each day to write in your journal. Trips can begin to blur together. By keeping a new journal each trip, you accumulate a written log of what you learned each time around.

The following reminders are also found in the team member's manual (chapter 6, pages 73-74). Keep the team as well as yourself focused on the big picture as these reminders suggest.

## THINGS TO REMEMBER WHILE ON THE TRIP

- *Remember why you are here:* Do you remember the reasons that prompted you to participate in this VWAP?
- *Remember your financial supporters:* Have you sent them a card?
- *Remember your prayer partner(s):* Are you praying for them in their life at home just as they are praying for you?

- *Remember your team leader(s):* Are you praying for and encouraging them?
- *Remember the other team members:* Is teamwork something you have been striving for?
- *Remember the nationals:* Has your interaction with them been marked by a servant's heart?
- *Remember a receptive heart and mind:* Have you been open and listening to how God is speaking to you through the events of each day?

Sometimes a little humor helps team members see where they might be getting off track. Rich Hurst made up this humorous list to point out problem areas to his team. (Page 74 of team member's manual.)

---

### TEN WAYS TO WRECK A GOOD TRIP

1. Act like you are there alone. Stay to yourself. Isolate others.
2. Think you are much too important for the work you have been assigned. If you are given dish duty, weasel out of it.
3. Don't pray or study the Bible. You won't have the time for it anyway.
4. Be well-organized and inflexible so nothing can interfere with your agenda.
5. Point out what your hosts are doing wrong. Help them "improve." Help them be more like you.
6. If you are single, try to become romantically involved with someone on the team. Try to be near that person, even if it means that other team relationships suffer. If you're married, get away frequently to spend time together and to discuss how you'd run things differently if you were the leaders.
7. Don't bother trying to speak the language. Seek out English speakers, then communicate only with them.
8. Point out the faults of people on your team. Try not to be seen with the socially awkward people on the team.
9. Make sure you don't eat the local food. Try to find a grocery store that sells something familiar. If you are forced to eat the local cuisine, complain.
10. Be generally disappointed in how things are going. Whine when things go wrong.

---

## GROWING AS A TEAM

There are a variety of ways to encourage personal growth in your team members. One group uses a *team journal*, which is left in an accessible area during the entire day. Throughout the day, team members slip by to jot down a thought or prayer. The team journal is also used to record significant issues discussed or shared in daily team meetings.

Other teams have *daily prayer partners*. In addition to ensuring that team members spend time with all the other team participants on a one-on-one basis, praying together also enhances the sense of community within the team. Each morning, put all the team members' names into a hat and draw them out in pairs. Encourage each pair to meet once that day to talk and pray with each other.

## Team Meetings

Time spent alone as a team, away from your host families, the local congregation, and the missionaries, is essential for a healthy VWAP. These team meetings give team members a chance to safely discuss their questions, observations, and concerns without embarrassing themselves or the hosts. These meetings also provide an important time for processing the spiritual implications of their experiences.

It's important that you clearly communicate to the hosts the need for daily private team meetings. Ask if they can provide a suitable meeting place for the team. Most teams find meeting in the evening is best. The team can gather after the day's work or activities to recap the day, discuss important matters, and have a team devotional.

## TEAM DEVOTIONALS

Team devotions can be handled any number of ways. The nature of your particular team will determine how your devotions operate. Three suggestions are listed here.

## Buddy System

Before departure choose devotion teams of two or three. New Christians and nonChristians should not be excluded; pair them with a more mature Christian. Each devotion team is responsible for organizing an evening's sharing, prayer, and praise. It is their responsibility to bring thought-provoking questions for discussion, and then keep the group from digressing, complaining, or gossiping during the group's interaction. The delightful benefit of team-led devotions is the diversity that each evening's team can bring: We've had everything from hymns to spirituals, from communion to M & M's. This is also a great way to give the quieter members a real sense of their importance to the team.

## Rotation

This format is the same as above, except that, instead of teams, different individuals lead each night's program. This alternative is necessary when pairs of team members do not have a chance to prepare and coordinate a devotional. When something is weighing heavily on the collective heart of the group, one team member may be asked to lead a spontaneous sharing time. Diversity can be wonderful: We've heard a storyteller dramatize the book of Esther, and cried together as a team member shared the fear and pain he felt because of the poverty around him. Devotions are a time to see the gifts of the Body at work.

## Team Pastor

This format works well when the "pastor" is thoroughly prepared. One person is chosen well ahead of time to prepare a series to be taught each night of the trip. Any member of the team who has maturity as a Christian, the will to do the preparation, and a good teaching style can be chosen. (Remember, the devotions often take place at the end of a long day, so a low-key, unprepared session can mean trouble.) Choose a series that will relate directly to the experiences of the trip and provide ample fuel for your discussion. The Bible study portion should help team members see how they can integrate their new experiences into their lives as Christians.

While time alone as a team is important, so is taking advantage of what your hosts can teach you. Some teams have invited the missionary or pastor to join them for one of their team meetings so they could hear the pastor's testimony, or the missionary's dreams. Keep an eye out for opportunities to invite a special guest to one of your meetings. Are there other things you can do to help team members grow in their faith and knowledge of the Lord Jesus Christ?

CHAPTER FIFTEEN

# BECOMING PART
# OF THE COMMUNITY

In chapter 10, we looked at ways teams can prepare to relate positively, humbly, and effectively with nationals. Upon arrival the lessons go into action. You've undoubtedly felt the tug of friendship from the nationals you've met. Perhaps you've been invited to attend church services, or even participate in them.

One team found that their trip included much more interaction with the congregation than they had anticipated. Each team member stayed in the home of a different family from the congregation and—except for the eight hours spent daily at the worksite—was expected to participate in that family's routine.

An important part of each family's routine was attending church services held every evening. At first team members did not look forward to the nightly meetings, the hard benches, and the struggle to understand words whispered by the team translator. However, they soon discovered these services were a great way to interact with the community and an appropriate complement to their workday. They even began to look forward to going.

Special presentations made by members of the congregation highlighted each evening meeting. At times it was special prayer, or a message spoken by a congregation member. On two occasions, the church's teenagers gave a musical performance which they had obviously spent a great deal of time preparing. The team members received this gracious display of appreciation with mixed feelings. On one hand, they were greatly honored and uplifted by the congregation's efforts. On the other hand, they wondered with increasing apprehension what they could do to reciprocate. Certainly the hard work they were offering each day was appreciated by the congregation, but they wished they could contribute something to the worship services.

The team decided to make a contribution to the final evening's service. One person chose to share his testimony. A small group of teammates practiced singing hymns in four-part harmony, each one trying to remember the appropriate notes without a hymnal. The whole group practiced a song they had learned before the trip so they could teach it to the congregation.

At that evening's service, as was his custom, the pastor asked the group if they wanted to lead part of the worship. To the pastor's surprise and delight, the answer was yes. The man who offered his testimony was delighted to find that the members of the congregation were eager to hear someone testify about his relationship with God, even though they didn't seem to comprehend the specific details of the story. The group that sang hymns realized many of their listeners were hearing four-part vocal harmony for the first time. And the whole team delighted in teaching the congregation a new chorus in their own language!

Teams have learned that one of the few expectations their hosts have include presenting songs, skits, and testimonies. Unfortunately, it's the thing we often feel least comfortable offering. The team member's manual (chapter 6, pages 75-76) contains the tips shown here for preparing testimonies. Before you leave, or shortly after you arrive, begin to prepare ways of sharing yourselves with the worshiping community. Give opportunities to as many team members as possible. Even the hesitant will find it a stretching and memorable experience.

## TIPS ON GIVING TESTIMONIES/PRESENTATIONS

In all likelihood you will be asked to share a brief testimony while on your VWAP. In our experience, the nationals enjoy hearing about what God is doing in the lives of individual team members. Since many people are unfamiliar with speaking in a different culture, we hope the following tips will be of assistance. Ask your leader to listen to your main thoughts before you give the testimony in a church service.

1. Remember, you may have a translator. You may have to pause quite frequently, depending on the skill of the translator. Use simple phrases and avoid slang, which is difficult to translate.
2. Avoid mentioning material possessions you have at home. For example, don't talk about how you learned to trust God when your Porsche was almost stolen!
3. Remember the particular culture. It may be inappropriate to discuss certain topics or activities. (For example, "I met my husband at a church dance.")
4. Keep it brief.
5. Possible subjects to cover are a brief spiritual autobiography or what God has been teaching you while you have been in the country.
6. Communicate your appreciation of the people, the church, the country, the culture.
7. Avoid making negative comparisons between the host culture and your own.
8. Avoid inside jokes between you and your teammates. They only confuse the nationals.
9. Dress properly for the worship service. Customs are not as lax in most other countries when it comes to church attire.
10. Reflect the role of a student instead of a teacher. Avoid large, sweeping

suggestions on how they could improve their country, or situation, or church.

11. Write down your main points before getting up. This keeps you from getting off on irrelevant tangents.

---

Use the space below to record your thoughts as you prepare your testimony. Your notes will be a reminder once you're home of the things you said.

---

In addition to hearing testimonies, church members often enjoy . . .

- songs in their language (you've learned a few);
- hymns and choruses in English, especially sung in harmony;
- puppet shows and mimes that communicate the message of the gospel; and
- *anything* else that has been carefully prepared and practiced for their benefit.

## SAYING GOOD-BY

Much sooner than you expect, the day will arrive to say good-by. This can be an emotionally wrenching time. It is important to prepare the team for this time of closure with the nationals. Review the following information (team member's manual, chapter 8, pages 95-96) with them a day or two prior to leaving for the vacation portion of the trip.

You may never have considered that this part of the trip would be difficult. But you are finding out it is. Good-bys are emotionally draining. They clearly signify the end of the trip. You are leaving friends you have grown to love and may never see again. For many of the hosts and team members, the good-bys are a tearful time.

On the last day, the things you have looked forward to returning to at home—friends, family, car, ice, flush toilets, etc.—may seem curiously distant and unimportant.

We have always found good-bys difficult. Perhaps the following items can help you keep your good-bys in perspective.

1. *Do not be afraid to show and express emotion.* More than likely the nationals have fewer inhibitions than you, so learn from them! Hugs and words of appreciation are expressions you will not regret.
2. *Treasure the moment.* So often we live our lives for the future and fail to appreciate the present moment. This is a good moment, one that cannot be duplicated. So be present and value what is happening.
3. *Get the addresses of those you intend to write.* Do not make commitments to everyone. Be realistic and that will help you have integrity at home and abroad.
4. *Give a small gift as a token of your friendship.* The giving of gifts should not be elaborate because that may introduce awkwardness into the friendship. Rather, choose something personal that will remind the person of you.
5. *Talk about your feelings with the team after you have departed.* This will create an environment where others may feel it's okay to share their grief and joy.
6. *Do not expect others to handle the good-bys as you do.* We all respond differently to emotionally charged events. Be accepting of others' ebullience or sorrow.
7. *Get plenty of photographs or video footage.* You (and perhaps only you) will value this once at home. You may also want to send photographs to the host community once you're home. (Be sure photographs and videos are appropriate in the host community.)
8. *Agree to pray for one another.* This is the most important expression of love you may be able to give your newfound friends. Let them know they will be in your prayers.
9. *Avoid making financial commitments during the good-by phase.* You may confuse a very valuable time by introducing finances into your farewells. Furthermore, you might make a commitment you are unable to keep once home. Wait and think through your financial decisions.

A leader can encourage the team members to reflect often on what it means to have been part of the host community. This memory will often leave the most lasting impression on the team.

Adopt an attitude of appreciation to the host community for sharing their lives with you and the team. In many ways, the building you built or the ministry you offered was the "rent" you paid for the privilege of having this community teach you about God, about themselves, and about you.

# CHAPTER SIXTEEN

# REST AND REFLECTION

From time to time throughout this book, we've referred to the R & R portion of the trip. This is the time set aside at the end of the trip, when team members can relax with one another and rest their aching muscles. All too soon they will be heading back to their own jobs or responsibilities. So this time is their much needed buffer between worlds. It is more than lying by the pool or shopping in open-air markets. The purpose of R & R is *rest* and *reflection*.

As the team leader, you'll be in a position to shape these last few days into an important time of debriefing and processing the events and lessons of the VWAP. You have the opportunity to build a bridge between the world the team members have been in for several days or weeks and the world to which they are returning. For many participants, this return to their "regular" world may be very difficult. To simply take them from one place to the other without attempting to help them integrate the experience is not only unfair but diminishes the potential impact the trip can have on others.

## GROUP REFLECTION EXERCISES

There are a number of things you can do during the R & R portion of the trip to help solidify the experience. Below are three ideas used by churches for their VWAP teams:

### The Empathy Circle

Through a VWAP experience, team members often learn to empathize and identify more closely with the lives of people they meet. This exercise is a good tool for encouraging them to place themselves in the circumstances of others. Have the team members sit in a circle and each one tell a three-minute story, in first-person narrative, about someone he or she knows whose life presents special challenges and difficulties. Often, though not always, the person whose identity the team member assumes is someone he or she met on the trip. (For example, "My name is Maria. I am the widowed mother of four children. . . ." [Spend three minutes telling Maria's story as a first-person narrative.]) Speaking as though they were that person, the team member tells what he or she knows about the other person's life, the triumphs as well as the tribulations. Each team member tells the story of a different person.

These stories give insights into the narrator as well as the individuals they portray. One of the tremendous benefits of a VWAP is the insight into nationals as well as team members. There is more to everyone than meets the eye. When each person has had a chance to share, close by praying for those people whose stories have just been told.

### Teammate Affirmations

One group assigns each person a "secret pal" by picking names from a hat on the first day of travel. During the trip, team members pray for their secret pal each day. If the team has the opportunity to buy souvenirs, each person buys an inexpensive gift for his or her secret pal. At one of the evening meetings on the R & R portion, team members reveal the identity of their secret pals and give three reasons they appreciated having that person on the trip.

### Communion Service

Many teams end their trip with a worship and communion service. The form the service takes varies, depending on denominational background, setting, and resources available. One church's teams head out to the beach on the morning of the last day for a time of singing, prayer, and "the breaking of the tortilla."

As the leader, you can do a great deal to foster an attitude of reflection and worship during the last few days. Encourage team members to go through the material found in their books. Let them know they are not alone in their feelings. Prepare them for the plethora of emotions they will feel once they are home. The whole debriefing and follow-up portions of a VWAP can be a great time for team members to become more open and honest with each other.

Shown below is a segment from the team member's manual (chapter 9). It contains comments designed to help them process their experience and share with others once they are home. *Be sure to familiarize yourself with the material prior to the R & R.* At an appropriate time—the last evening or last meal together—use this material for a group discussion. Help team members come up with practical ways they can apply the experience to their everyday lives (see chapter 17, page 168, for a list of suggestions). This is a good time to utilize team members who have been on teams before. Ask them to share some of the experiences they had leaving their first VWAP and going home.

It is hard to believe, but it is just about time to begin traveling home. Back to "regular" life . . . although at this point you may not be sure exactly what that is!

A mistake many participants make is assuming they will be able to jump easily from one world into the next, to go from this experience into the nine-to-five routine. There needs to be an adjustment period. Allow yourself the freedom to have it. The following material will help you think through the reality of entering life back at home. Be sure to talk through these tips with others on your team. (See team member's manual, pages 99-100.)

## TIPS FOR ENTERING LIFE BACK HOME

*Don't expect too much from other people.* People may be too busy to listen to you as much as you expect them to. They won't be as excited about your trip as you are (not even your close family and friends). Remember, they had their own experiences while you were gone. Keeping your expectations low allows you to be pleasantly surprised by those who show great interest.

*Share briefly.* People do not want to hear everything that happened to you. Stifle the tendency to take them through a day-by-day account. They'll lose interest about midway through the second day!

*Be careful about value judgments.* Do not argue with people about values. It is counterproductive and alienates them. Upon your return, you may tend to be judgmental about the values in American culture. We all need to reevaluate our lifestyles from time to time, but it's not up to us to determine others' convictions for them. The Holy Spirit is far more effective than a censorious spirit. Let them see a changed life.

*Do not be critical of others' spirituality.* God may be teaching others in ways you do not understand. Just because you went on this trip and learned what you did does not give you the right to be critical of others.

*Be prepared for nostalgia.* Sometimes you may long to be back in the country. You may ache to be back with some of the nationals who became your friends. And believe it or not, you may even want to be back with some of your teammates! Expect those feelings and be prepared for them.

*Don't let a little depression take you by surprise.* When feelings of nostalgia hit, you may experience a little depression. Others go through it, too, so call a teammate and talk with him or her about what you are feeling. Remember, you are not alone!

*Be cautious about negative reporting.* Things may have happened on your trip that were not to your liking. They are fresh in your mind now, but time will give you perspective on them. If you are very critical and negative in your reporting, you do a disservice to others and the VWAP. Share the tough experiences in light of what God taught you and the team through them.

*Try to stay in touch with one or two individuals you met on your trip.* Receiving a letter may help you remember the good experiences you had.

*Contact your prayer partners and financial supporters.* Of all the people back home, these will be the most interested in your trip. We suggest you make this contact as personal as your situation allows. Thank them for their prayers and support. Ask them to pray for you as you readjust to daily living.

*Develop some realistic, practical applications for yourself.* Avoid making unreasonable demands on yourself like, "I am going to pray for every missionary in that country for an hour every day." Think through some realistic ways of integrating your experiences into your daily routine at home.

## EVALUATING THE TRIP

The forms section of this book contains an evaluation form (pages 213-216) that team members can use to offer feedback on their trip. Before the trip starts, make one copy of the form for each member of the group, then take the blank copies with you on the trip. Sometime before the beginning of the R & R portion of the trip, carefully read over the questions. Use the space provided at the end to list any additional questions you would like to ask the team members.

### Why Use Evaluations?

Evaluations help in the planning of future teams. Who better to give input than those who were on the team? There may be ways to make the next trip even better, and these evaluations will provide the necessary input. In addition, the information in the evaluations may be of value to your hosts or hosting agency. We have found agencies very receptive to hearing both positive and negative feedback.

### What to Look For

Look for continuing themes throughout the evaluations. Leaders tend to focus on one or two random statements made in the evaluations. However, do not put too much emphasis on random comments. Rather, pick out ones mentioned again and again. For example, if "Teamwork" or "Exposure to the Culture" received a low overall score, spend time examining the reasons why.

Look for new ideas in the section that asks how the team could have been better prepared. This is where you will find suggestions for future teams, as well as weaknesses in your training program.

Last, note the differences (if any) between the answers of first-timers and VWAP veterans. Is there any consistency in their comments?

### How to Administer Evaluations

Team members will ask if they can fill out the evaluations once they return home. Our experience has shown us that, when a leader allows this, not all evaluations get returned. We suggest you have the team do their evaluations during the trip home. Explain the importance of their input and discourage them from rushing through the items. When the forms are completed, collect them, put them in an envelope, and forget about them until you are home.

*Important:* We recommend that the team leader(s) not read the evaluations. Reading a negative comment from one person can send a tired leader over the edge. Team members will feel they can be more honest if the evaluations will not be read by the person(s) they are evaluating.

Once the VWAP planning team (or church staff liaison) has read through the evaluations, we suggest they put together a one-page synopsis of the evaluations. This should include overall comments and/or scores from each of the questions on the sheet. This synopsis will be very helpful for the leaders and will help facilitate the evaluation.

If a member of your leadership team received very negative evaluations consider getting together with him or her individually to discuss the problem.

Evaluations can be very, very helpful, but they can also be very hurtful. If there has been friction between a team member and a team leader, the member may use the evaluation as an opportunity to "blast" away at the leader. *Be sure to get the leader's story as well as the team member's.*

Again, do not become overly depressed by negative evaluations. Remember, this is a learning process; with each VWAP team, a church gains a little more knowledge.

# PART FIVE

# ONCE THE TEAM IS HOME

*We may tend to think that once the team is home the leader's job is finished. "I got them home safely . . . now I'm done." But in reality, the most significant part of the leader's job has just begun! This is the opportunity to help team participants incorporate into their lives the things they have learned. It is also the time to encourage them in the sharing of their experience with those around them.*

CHAPTER SEVENTEEN

# FOLLOWING UP

We did not expect the individual team members to train themselves or organize their trip, so why should we expect them to follow up on themselves? Yet that is exactly how many churches run their Vacations with a Purpose programs.

By having some follow-up time with the participants, the leaders help team members work through what they have seen, heard, touched, felt, thought, and learned. It also encourages them to make ongoing responses to their experience. They begin to understand that this was not just a one-or-two-week vacation, but rather an event with the potential to change their life, and perhaps the lives of those around them.

There is a section later in this chapter (and in the team member's manual, beginning on page 103) entitled "Back-at-Home Study Material," page 160. The questions it contains direct team members through a personal evaluation of their time on the field. As team leader, you may wish to complete the material and use it as a guideline for team discussions.

The following are ideas for follow-up meetings that we have seen work very well.

## Back-at-Home Team Meeting
Most team members go through tremendous withdrawal the first few days back at home. Gone is the constant, loving community. Gone are the only others who can really understand what the experience meant. Gone is the euphoria of having such a strong sense of purpose, even if for only a few days. To help team members deal with the sense of loss they feel, arrange a team meeting about one week after their return. The team members will appreciate seeing their teammates and having the chance to discuss their feelings with others who can understand.

## Slide/Photograph/Video Party
This can be combined with the meeting described above, or it can be strictly a social get-together. Team members might even invite their friends to be part of the evening. Team members will enjoy seeing one another's pictures, ordering reprints, and laughing over happy memories. Some teams use this

occasion to have "secret pals" exchange gifts and publicly affirm one another. (See chapter 16, page 152, for more on this.) Follow the pictures/slides with a short challenge or sharing time.

### Discussion and Study Times

Teams use these get-togethers to talk over and work through common concerns. The material at the back of this chapter, page 168 (chapter 10, pages 112-113, in the team member's manual), provides good fuel for discussion.

### Yearly Meeting of VWAP Participants

Schedule this event for the end of the year and include all the VWAPers who went out from your church that year. If possible, seat people around tables of eight or so. Each table should include people representing each team. Spend the dinner time in informal discussion and sharing about the similarities and differences between the different trips. Follow that with a slide program from each group's trip, songs from the countries visited, and prayer for the missionaries and nationals that you came to know. Following that, have the people turn back to their tables for group discussion. Some tables might make the decision as a group to begin supporting or writing to a missionary or national. Others may make plans to become involved in a Third-World ministry.

### Presentation Planning Meetings

Chances are, your group will be asked to give a presentation at one of your church gatherings. Planning meetings for these presentations is another great way to do team follow-up. As team members get involved in telling their story to others, they continue to grow in what they learned.

### BACK-AT-HOME STUDY MATERIAL

The following material is meant to help you think through the entire VWAP experience. You may tend to procrastinate because things are so busy once you are home. However, to maximize what you have experienced on your trip, take time during your first month home to work through this material. We also suggest discussing this material with at least one other team member.

The trip that was the focus of so much energy, time, and money is over. Went by quickly, didn't it? Does it seem like only yesterday that you were looking through the "What to Bring" list and frantically running out to the discount store to get all the little necessities? Remember wondering how in the world you would ever get everything packed in *just* two suitcases? You needed a miracle on the scale of the parting of the Red Sea!

If you are like others who have gone, you are probably experiencing a wide range of emotions and thoughts at this time. There's a sense of loneliness now that you are not with your team members twenty-four hours a day (and perhaps a sense of thankfulness, too!). It felt good to have friends around who were experiencing many of the same things. There was always someone to share and pray and laugh with. There's a sense of having touched something very real and significant. And there is the question of what it all means to your everyday life. You may feel the need to do something with your experience. But what form should it take? Lastly, there can be an enormous amount of exhaustion creating a desire, at least for the moment, to file away this "missions stuff" or "world need stuff."

Now, while things are still fresh in your mind, is the time to process your experience. Think through what you saw while in the country and with the people. Reflect on the situations in which you lived and served. Go back and try to relive the feelings you had when you were confronted with needs. How did you feel about yourself and your life? Thinking through the trip will help you focus on the main issue you face at home: What will be your response now that you are back?

A VWAP experience is a special gift. Yes, you had a hand in making it happen. But more than likely, a number of things came together to make your participation possible. Wasn't God the One who orchestrated your going? Why did He choose you? Is this unique "vacation" simply another experience to be filed away in your memory banks? Chances are high that if you take time to reflect on and analyze your trip you will find much that could radically impact your lifestyle and choices. But that's a big *if*. Some come back and figure they'll think about it "one of these days." All too quickly they get caught up in the pace and stress of daily living. They are too busy to draw all they could out of the trip. Ignore, for the moment, a few of the daily demands on your time and draw away and allow God to guide you in understanding the implications of your trip. Do it *now*.

The following four sections will help you in that process. Please do them in the order given and avoid the tendency to rush. Keep in mind that you are doing this for yourself—no one else. Make an appointment with yourself to do each section in the next two weeks.

The euphoria will eventually evaporate. The daily routine gradually disperses it. But it's not the euphoric feelings that are going to matter six months or a year from now. What matters are the memories, and the lessons, and the choices that were precipitated by your VWAP.

## WHAT I SAW

Begin by remembering the different things you saw on the trip—both the expected and the unexpected.

One thing is for sure: Your eyes were *open* while you were there. Does that sound like a ridiculous statement? How could one's eyes not be open? Yet very often in our everyday lives we go through our routines and never "see" things. We are too busy or too preoccupied to notice them. But it was different on your trip; you had prepared yourself to "see." You were determined to observe the various things you would encounter each day. Take some time now to reflect upon what you saw.

**The People**

1. What did you see in the people that you did not expect to see?

2. Which of their needs are most vivid in your memory?

3. What aspects of their lives impressed you most?

**The Country**

4. What things did you see in the country that were different from your expectations?

5. Is there any picture that quickly comes to mind? (Briefly describe it and the reasons it has stayed with you.)

Seeing is a discipline we develop. It is the first step in making a difference in our world. Unless one sees the needs, one can never meet the needs.

Because you were willing to keep your eyes open on the trip, you probably "saw" quite a bit. Not merely sights and sounds all jumbled together, but needs, issues, and concerns festering beneath the surface. We hope that what you saw will stick with you and, more importantly, you will continue to keep your eyes open.

Jesus admonished the disciples to "open their eyes and see," an admonition well suited for His disciples today as well. So many Christians live without ever really seeing. Perhaps you were one of them before this trip. Now the question is not only whether you will remember what you saw in the countries you were in, but whether you will continue to "see" each and every day.

6. What keeps you from "seeing" in your world?

## WHAT I LEARNED

As your experience in and knowledge of the host country has grown, perhaps some ignorance in your perspective about the world and its inhabitants has been dispelled. We hope you took time to listen and learn from those you encountered. Take time to reflect upon what you have learned.

7. List two things you learned about each of the following:

a. The people

b. The country

c. The church in the country

d. The people on your team

e. Yourself

8. Which of the above surprised you? Why?

9. Look back over the needs you noted "seeing" (question 2) and rephrase them here.

Needs do not simply appear out of nowhere. Rather, there are factors that contribute to their existence. If we understand these factors, we are better able to identify with the people and work with them in meeting their needs.

10. What factors have contributed to the needs of the people you were with? (Think through the sociological, political, spiritual, emotional, and physical factors you may have heard about.)

Understanding our world requires effort. Far too often, people put forth no effort to become educated to the situations around them. Seeing needs is a necessary beginning, but without understanding what we see we can be of little help. The question for you is, now that you have seen and understood the people's needs, will your life be the same as it had been before the trip?

11. What keeps people from learning about and understanding the needs in their world?

## WHAT I FELT

The writers of the gospels tell us that whenever Jesus Christ encountered people in need He was deeply moved by what He saw. He felt the pain of their need and situation. During your time in the country there were probably situations that caused you to feel deeply. As you saw a particular person or an incident, you may have been "deeply moved." In those times you were most likely being challenged by God in some way.

12. a. Think of at least one situation on your trip when you really "felt deeply" about something. Write a description of the situation.

    b. What was it you "felt"? (Try to describe the feelings you had at that moment.)

    c. Were you surprised by your feelings? Why?

13. As you reflect back on that situation, what growth do you think God had in mind for you in those feelings?

Feelings come and go, there's no doubt about that. Yet, the feelings you experienced on this trip may be etched in your memory forever. And their memory may prompt you to feel deeply again and again in the world in which you live. God meant for you to go on this trip. And He will continue to challenge you to grow. Will you pay Him the same sort of attention now as you did on your trip? He is not through with you yet.

14. What factors may prevent you from being "deeply moved" in the world in which you live?

## HOW I WILL RESPOND

Now comes the tough but exciting part: the application of what you saw, learned, and felt. What are you going to do with your experience? How are you going to respond to the things God is teaching you?

It is one thing to go on a trip and have a great time. Many do. But it is quite another to go on a trip and allow the experience to change you and the world in which you live. The process of responding is an ongoing one that requires you to make decisions day by day. It requires ongoing action. Your trip only began a process. The process is not finished. In this section, instead of reflecting on the trip, think about the present.

15. a. What changes have you made in your life as a result of what you have seen, learned, and felt on this trip?

b. Why those changes?

16. Think in terms of three areas of possible ongoing responses to the world you live in.

   a. How might you use your time differently based on what you have experienced?

   b. How might you use your money or resources differently based on what you have experienced?

   c. How might you adjust your lifestyle based on what you have experienced?

17. What ideas do you have for remembering the people you met and the experiences you had?

## SUGGESTED WAYS TO STAY INVOLVED ONCE YOU RETURN

The previous questions will help you think about your response in general terms. Now, think about specific responses. The following are just a few ways former VWAP participants have integrated the experience into their lives.

*Mission committee membership and/or participation in the church's mission conference.* One team member had never considered being involved in any of his church's mission activities. After his VWAP, he became active on committees and educated himself about the concerns in areas where his church's missionaries were working. He also began contributing more of his monthly income to missions.

*Further language study.* One woman, after a trip to the Dominican Republic, investigated language classes at a local junior college. She decided to enroll and study Spanish in the hopes of being able to communicate more effectively the next time she traveled in Spanish-speaking areas.

*Involvement with international students through local universities or ministries to international students.* This is a great opportunity to return the hospitality shown you by your host community. Many international students want to experience North American homes and ways of life.

*Monthly support of a child through a child sponsorship agency.* Nancy began sponsoring a child at an orphanage in Mexico. The relationship grew to be more than merely a financial one, however. In the ensuing years she made several trips to the orphanage to spend time with the child. In addition, visitors to Nancy's apartment quickly notice the numerous photographs and letters from her special little girl.

*Further study of the religious, economic, social, and political situations related to the host culture.* This is often done by former participants who, as North American Christians, want to increase their understanding of the host culture so they can respond appropriately to important issues.

*Involvement in local community ministries.* Holly participated on a team that worked at a school for the deaf. As a direct result of her experience, she changed her major in college to deaf communications and is currently working as a liaison between the state government and the local deaf community.

*Writing notes of encouragement and praying for missionaries and host community members.* Many VWAP participants, who hardly concerned themselves with the lives and work of missionaries or people of other cultures prior to their trip, became very active in the support of missionaries and nationals through their money, prayer, and correspondence.

*Involvement in longer-term, cross-cultural missionary service.* One team member joined a VWAP to investigate her sense of being called by God to serve overseas. She took one day off from the work site to interview with a mission agency operating in the city where she was interested in utilizing her gifts as a teacher. Six months later, she was back in the country as a missionary.

# CHAPTER EIGHTEEN

# FINAL DETAILS

Well, tired team leader, your job is almost done! But not quite. You've led your team through the preparation and the on-field and follow-up portions of the VWAP. Now it's time for *you* to be debriefed. Before you sit down to be debriefed by the planning committee, take time to answer these questions.

1. What could have made this VWAP better? For you? For the team members? For the host community? For the missionary?

2. What was the hardest thing you faced as a leader?

3. If you could give one piece of advice to a future leader, what would it be?

4. Did you feel well prepared? How could you have been better prepared?



5. Could you have been better supported? In what way?

## DEBRIEFING LEADERS

Sometime within two weeks of your return home, meet with the planning committee and discuss your answers to the foregoing questions. In addition, use the meeting to tie up the following loose ends.

*Evaluations:* You will have collected the team's evaluations and given them, unread, to the planning committee. They will give you the team members' feedback about the trip and your leadership of it.

*Your Evaluation of the Team:* It will be helpful for the planning committee to hear or read the leader's evaluation of the team members, the project, the hosts, the missions agency, the lodging, the touring, the finances, and so on. The team leaders are the church's best source of information on how things went.

*Designating Potential Leaders from the Team:* While abroad, you observed team members in both easy and difficult situations. You are familiar with the character of the participants and therefore can offer invaluable counsel regarding leadership, not only for future teams, but for church positions as well.

*Finish Accounting Chores:* Tally the accounts and turn in any leftover funds. Keeping exact records will help you with future team pricing. Do not procrastinate on closing the books for this trip. Close out the account while it is still fresh in your mind.

*Final Record of Trip:* After meeting with you, the leadership team should type up a synopsis of the trip. Keep this on file for the planning of future teams; it will be a very valuable resource. One final word on recordkeeping: *Do not* throw away any of the correspondence, receipts, or promotional material for the team. Your records provide very useful information for future teams.

## COMMUNICATING THE EXPERIENCE TO OTHERS

Your last job is to help your team members prepare to share their trip with others. The team member's manual (chapter 11, pages 114-115) contains the information you have here, which tells them (and you) how to effectively communicate their experience. As team leader, you may wish to review the information with them at one of your follow-up get-togethers.

### Church Presentations

Chances are, you and your team will be asked to give a presentation at your church. (If you are not asked, make the offer to the appropriate people.) Remember, the more effectively you communicate about your trip, the more likely others will want to be involved in the future.

1. *Use slides when possible.* Visual aids help communicate what you saw and experienced. However, be careful not to overdo it. Some may be delighted you took 500 pictures, but their delight does not translate into a desire to see all 500! Show only as many as necessary to communicate your trip. As a trial run, show your slides to a non-team member prior to a big presentation. One group puts the slides to music and produces an interesting and moving multimedia presentation. Since they use several projectors, they can use more slides and still keep the whole presentation moving along quickly.
2. *Keep it short and to the point.* People do not want a day-by-day, feeling-by-feeling, meal-by-meal account of the trip. They were not there and cannot possibly comprehend every aspect of your experience. Boring them will be a turnoff to the whole idea of VWAP.
3. *Focus on how your life is different because of what you have seen and experienced.* People find that to be both interesting and challenging.
4. *Communicate appreciation for being able to go.* Do not come across as arrogant or self-righteous. These people more than likely helped provide you with the opportunity.
5. *Do not preach.* As anyone in the church knows, we have enough fine preachers. What we often need are peers who share their lives and insights with us.

### Common Mistakes

The list below includes the most common complaints teams have heard from the audiences about their presentations:

- The team put too many expectations on the presentation.
- It was too long!
- There were too many slides, or too much *unedited* video.
- It was too team-oriented. The team wasn't thinking about their audience.
- The team was too demanding. They wanted everyone to have some

sort of response to their message (trying to play Holy Spirit).
• There was too much criticism of our own culture.
• They were too critical of Christianity at home.
• There was too much talk and too little action.

## Financial Supporters and Prayer Partners

Your financial supporters and prayer partners will be the most interested group. Remember, they invested in it. It is a mistake to neglect them once you are home. Very often we run to tell our friends about the trip and show them the pictures, but we neglect to run to our supporters. Then we wonder why they're not all that interested in becoming involved in a VWAP in the future. Keep in mind that your trip is partially owned by them. You were the one who was able to go, but they had a part in making it happen.

Communicating to these people is also a great opportunity for you to broaden their interest in world need. You may well be their closest contact to the global community. By sharing your experience, people in different cultures/countries become more than just images on a TV screen. Do not underestimate this potential.

The following are suggestions that others have used. Use these as a springboard for your own creative ideas.

1. *Send a letter to all supporters.* Include at least one photo of the people, the work, the church, or some significant event. Personalize these as much as possible to avoid the appearance of a form letter.
2. *Bring back little gifts for your supporters.* These do not need to be elaborate, but simply something from the culture. Everyone enjoys and appreciates getting a small token of appreciation.
3. *Have a dinner party and invite supporters to view your slides/photographs/video.* Some people have even attempted to cook a national dish and serve it.
4. *Share with them not only what you did and learned but what you intend to do with the experience.* Communicate the applications you intend to make to your life.
5. *Communicate to them how they might become involved.* Gently and sensitively share challenges with them. (If they are financial supporters, be cautious about asking for money again so soon.)

The future of the VWAP endeavor at your church depends a great deal on your close attention to the closure of this experience. Team members need debriefing. The church and supporters must be enfolded in the experience so it becomes something they continue to own. Meetings and letters and accounts all matter. The results of a thorough job will be felt for years to come.

# CHAPTER NINETEEN

# QUESTIONS ASKED MOST FREQUENTLY

### 1. Wouldn't it be better to just send the money directly to the project?

Often in the process of raising money, team members hear this question from their potential supporters. This is a valid question. It is true that by taking the money raised for a project and adding to it the funds required to send people on a VWAP we would be able to fund more of the project. However, it's important to keep two things in mind.

First, participation in the project is the vehicle for fund raising. It is doubtful that a group could raise as much in project funds were it not for their own physical participation. Second, and more importantly, our primary objective for a team is the personal and spiritual growth of the participants and the members of the congregations they represent. Hands-on involvement by individuals and congregation facilitates the development of "World Christians." In the long run, far more money is raised for missions when team members return having caught a vision for the financial concerns of mission agencies and national churches. Then they begin to give away more of their incomes.

### 2. How early should I start planning for a VWAP?

Allow at least six months advance planning. You can figure on needing at least six weeks to select the site, three months for promotion and team selection, and six weeks for team training.

### 3. How necessary are language skills?

Probably not as necessary as people may think. While having one or two bilinguals on your team is a great relief to the hosts, the hosts are usually prepared to provide a translator. Make sure you make these arrangements early in your planning.

This does not mean that the team should not practice the language before going. It is important to learn some of the basics. The curriculum in chapter 11 gives a good idea how much training is adequate (pages 118-125). However, a lack of language skills should not discourage one from pursuing a VWAP.

## 4. What if I am excited about the idea of VWAP, but other leaders in my church are not?

Inspiring them may take some time, perseverance, and patience. We would suggest the following ideas:

- Pray about the possibilities prior to talking to the church leaders.
- Approach the appropriate leaders. Sometimes ignoring the proper leadership may jeopardize your whole endeavor.
- Get a hearing with the leaders who can make decisions.
- Present a coherent vision. Explain why you want to see this happen, what the benefits would be, and so on.
- Explain what you are willing to do and what you would expect from the church.
- Incorporate the leaders into the planning procedures.
- Wait.

## 5. Should nonChristians go on a team?

This decision is particular to each sending church. The authors both have had nonChristians on their teams. If they are comfortable with and understand the objectives, purposes, and goals of the trip, we do not see a problem. Often their interest signifies that something (perhaps spiritual hunger) is developing in their life. Their participation can be a great opportunity for the leader, the team, and the nonChristians.

## 6. What if a team member wants to take his or her child(ren)?

This has worked in the past, but it depends on the dynamics of a particular group. One important thing is to be sure all parties understand who will be responsible for the care of the child during the day. Is the team expected to take turns with child care? What are your expectations of the hosting community? The child's health or medical need may also be a factor.

## 7. What about physically handicapped members on a team?

A person's physical condition should serve as only one of several considerations. It is not the major factor for participation on a team. More often than not, such a person has developed valuable characteristics which more than compensate for his or her physical limitations. Depth of character as well as spiritual and mental vitality are frequently a greater asset to the team than sheer physical strength. Not surprisingly, participants with physical limitations often have a tremendous impact on team members and the host community. Nevertheless, logistics are a central consideration when assessing an applicant with physical limitations. For example, how much walking will the team be doing? What special provisions would be required? Does this person fully understand what he or she is getting into? Ultimately the final decision rests with the leadership team's appraisal of both the difficulties of the trip and the abilities and resources of the individual in question. Last but not least, the team must not overdo any special treatment or recognition of such a team member. Few behaviors are more irritating to someone with physical limitations than to be singled out with unnecessary concern or praise.

## 8. What if someone who has been on one VWAP wants to go on another?

It is not unusual for team members to want to take a second or third trip. These repeaters can become either an asset or a headache to the team leader. The repeat team member should keep the following things in mind:

- Don't compare this team/trip with your previous one. (Comparisons are not always helpful, wise, or constructive. Keep your comparisons to yourself. There will be time after you return to discuss and evaluate what you have learned from your consecutive trips.)
- Allow first-timers to experience VWAP at their own pace.
- Avoid trying to run the team.
- Prepare yourself for a completely new experience.
- Attend all classes and team meetings even if you are already familiar with some of the material.
- Assist the leader in the little things (e.g., baggage, minor travel details, etc.).
- Offer assistance to the team as a resource person (about cultural courtesies, etc.), but do not act like a know-it-all.
- Examine your motive for going. Are you trying to duplicate your last experience?

We recommend going through these items with repeat team members. Be sure to take the time to do this. This may prevent problems, regulate expectations, and ensure a positive experience.

## 9. What if a team member does not attend the preparation meetings?

This can be a tough call. A leader must first establish the reasons behind the team member's absence. A person with an erratic work schedule or traveling responsibilities may be unable to attend every session. These absences must be discussed with the team leader. Furthermore, he or she is responsible to catch up on material missed and be aware of the lost opportunity for team building.

If a team member simply skips meetings, you have a different problem. When someone blatantly ignores the requirement to participate in team meetings, be assured that this behavior will continue on the field and hurt everyone's experience. If, after sitting down and talking together, you find the person is truly unwilling to participate as a team player and operate within the framework of the covenant, you may need to exclude this person from the trip.

Unavoidable absences require both flexibility and a plan for make-up assignments.

### 10. What if a team member fails to raise all the necessary funds?

This depends on the group's policies. Did the team member understand that he or she was primarily responsible for raising the funds? Or did the team member think the church would "bail" him or her out?

Usually, if a team member goes through all the preparation classes and works hard at raising the funds but comes up short, other team members will help him or her out. However, it is important early in the process to clearly define whose responsibility the fund raising is.

### 11. What if a team member wants to alter his or her travel plans, either arriving early or staying late?

First, consider the logistics. Check with your travel agent to make sure that your group discounts will not be affected by alternate travel arrangements for one or more members of your group. How feasible is a rendezvous in the host country? Are you miles from an airport? Is transportation available and dependable?

Second, think through the issue of team dynamics. Important group dynamics develop during the trip to the site. The initial plane ride and any subsequent travel are important venues for molding your group into a team.

Remaining behind after the team leaves is another issue. Our trips have generally run from ten days to two weeks because that's all the vacation time people have. But some of our team members who have more time express a desire to stay in the country for additional days. We have found that certain guidelines are useful in this case.

- Those desiring to stay must make their intentions known well before the team's tickets are purchased and must agree to make their alternate arrangements with the group's travel agent.
- They must realize that the team leader's responsibility for them ends when they part company with the team. This also applies to any responsibility the mission organization may have had.
- They must stay with the team for the entire time the team is together on the field, including the R & R portion at the end of the trip.

### 12. Do you have to have an R & R portion?

We highly recommend it. An R & R portion enables the team to have some rest and relaxation before returning to their jobs—after all, for many participants this may be their only vacation time all year. In addition, the R & R portion gives the team time to process their experience before arriving home.

It is a bridge between two worlds. It is the leader's responsibility to use the debriefing material, mealtime discussions, and travel time to keep the team's focus on their experience and how it will apply to life back home.

### 13. How much sightseeing/touring is too much?

More than two or three days on a ten to fourteen day trip would probably be viewed as extravagant by most team members. However, if you are near a beach, do not wait until the last day to enjoy it. Team members will appreciate cooling off each day, especially if they are doing a work project.

### 14. What about worried relatives?

This situation seems to arise no matter which country you go to. There are always people who will be worried about their adult children or relatives. This problem intensifies when you go to an area with known turmoil and political difficulties.

Be sure you have up-to-date information and news from the hosting country. *The better informed your team members are, the more likely they will be to relieve the fears of their relatives and friends.* In addition, be very clear and specific on where the team is staying, where the team is traveling, how they are traveling, what they will be doing in the evenings, etc. This shows concerned relatives that you're thinking through the team's itinerary beforehand and will not be "winging it."

If relatives, and specifically parents, are worried, strongly encourage VWAP participants to maintain contact on the field and while traveling (either through phone or mail, or if available, facsimile machines).

### 15. What if on-field meetings are not going well?

We have noticed a direct correlation between physical exhaustion and untalkative people in meetings. If you notice it in your group, you may want to change the meeting time to be more conducive for sharing.

Another suggestion is to change the present format of your meetings. Doing something completely different from the usual approach may help. Allow more team members to lead the meetings, or use music or small groups, and so on.

### 16. When should I make the decision to send someone home?

Sending someone home is never, and should never be, an easy decision. However, several situations require the team leader to consider this action.

*Illness:* Even if the team member is asking to stay, you should send him or her home when medical facilities are inadequate to handle an illness or injury. Do not take unnecessary risks. Don't allow people to act like "heroes."

*Insulting the Nationals:* Lovingly explain to the team member how his or her words or actions are offending the nationals. At this point a change in behavior must be evident or sending the person home becomes the only option. We do not want to create lasting damage to the work of the Church in that country.

***Inappropriate Relational Behavior:*** This is a rather broad category, but we're speaking mainly of immoral activity or inappropriate sexual advances, which hurt the team's unity. This applies to repeated inappropriate behavior toward nationals as well.

***Rebellion Against Leadership:*** If a person simply refuses to listen to anyone, it becomes rather obvious he or she cannot function as a team member. Leaders have few other options when this occurs.

We have found that in most cases (we're talking about adults, after all), problems such as those listed above can be talked out. This will require the leader(s) to be confrontative with the difficult person and honestly lay out the situation. Before departing for the trip, make sure team members clearly understand that they may be sent home and what situations may lead to such a decision.

When you find you must send someone home, contact your church office and thoroughly inform your superiors of the situation *prior* to the team member's return. Do not let the returning person be the only one to explain what has transpired. His or her story may be quite a bit different from the one you report when you get home.

### 17. What if the project is delayed due to extenuating circumstances (weather, political turmoil, shortage of materials)?

Sit them out. Realize the team may develop some attitude problems and be prepared to help draw those out. Remind the team that God is in control. Would we doubt His control if the conditions were favorable to what we wanted to do? Use the time to pray for the situation and the others it affects.

This is also a great time to spend with the nationals, since they are probably immobilized as well. Make the most of this opportunity for a cross-cultural experience.

### 18. What do you do if there are relational conflicts between team members?

Refer everyone back to the material on team dynamics. Sit down with the parties involved and encourage them to talk it out. Help them resolve their conflict. Discuss the issues, the possible solutions, and clear up any misunderstandings. Having team members pray for or with a different team member each day is a great way to ease some of these potential tensions. One group prepares ahead of time by "role-playing" conflicts that may arise. The team develops skills in conflict resolution as part of their preparation.

### 19. Should we take something special for the missionary hosts?

Definitely. This is always a kind token of appreciation for their hospitality. Ask the contact overseas if there are any items you could pick up for them. Certain goods cost much more overseas than they do here. It is much cheaper to carry items down than for the missionary or national to have them mailed. We have taken everything from children's Christmas gifts to a Big Mac!

### 20. What if you feel overwhelmed by all the necessary logistical details?

This is where some advance planning comes in. Allow yourself enough time to lay the foundation before beginning the trip. However, if you are already into it and feel overwhelmed, that piece of advice does you no good! Think through the areas that overwhelm you. Can you delegate some of the responsibilities? Are you allowing the team members to have some ownership (some responsibility)? Could you arrange for an assistant leader? Watch out for the do-it-yourself tendency that many leaders develop. Also, think of any outside people you may be able to call upon for assistance (e.g., former missionaries or overseas workers, pastors, or agencies specializing in VWAPs).

# EPILOGUE

As we look ahead, we wonder about the future of short-term mission teams. Will this movement invigorate missions and build God's Church? Or will the consequences of so many Americans abroad be detrimental?

We can envision two possible scenarios. With mounting apprehension, we can imagine this movement gaining momentum among churches in North America (and even on other continents) but leaving havoc in its wake. Will a day arrive when thousands of teams of adults overrun communities and cities around the world, selfishly attempting to obtain a spiritual high? The harm created would affect the sending church, the hosting community, and even the team members. Worse yet, if insensitively handled, short-term mission projects could result in further exploitation of the "have-nots" by well-meaning "haves" seeking adventure and vicarious fulfillment. The potential for damage could mitigate all the benefits.

But we can also envision a brighter scenario, offering a vision filled with possibilities. We can imagine thousands of teams in host communities around the world actually functioning as the Body of Christ—building and bearing one another up. Teachability and servanthood would be the marks of the teams. We see adults equipped to interact with love and sacrifice toward their brothers and sisters abroad. The entire venture would lead the members to a deeper understanding of what it means to call oneself a follower of Jesus Christ in the age of the global village. What happens across the sea, as well as how choices are made at home, begin to matter for the Kingdom's sake. Lives and lifestyles are changed both at home and abroad.

We realize the second vision is a high and idealistic one. But the two of us firmly believe that such a goal can be wholeheartedly embraced by churches both here and abroad.

# PART SIX
# APPENDICES

# MY JOURNAL

The next several pages are for keeping a record of the new things you are seeing, learning, and feeling. (Chapter 7, beginning on page 80, in the team member's manual.) Each day's entry includes a suggested Scripture reading, a question for your reflection, a record of the day's events, and a place for you to write your thoughts. The Scripture study and reflection questions are simply to prompt your journal writing. If you want to write down other things, feel free to do so. The better you can identify what you are feeling and learning, the more you will appreciate your journal later.

The journal has entries for a fourteen-day trip. Your trip may be longer or shorter. If it's shorter, consider skipping to days thirteen and fourteen for the last two days' entries. If it's longer, consider taking along a devotional guide.

Try to find time each day to enter something. Remember, your journal should answer the question "What happened *in* me today?" more than "What happened *to* me?" When the trip is over, reflect back often and thank God for the things He has shown you.

## DAY ONE

Today's Date

Place

What I/we did today:

❖ ❖ ❖

**For Personal Devotion**
*God knows all about me.* (Read Psalm 139.)

**For Personal Reflection**
Fuller Seminary missions professor Dr. Tom Brewster used to say that no matter what you may think, you *can* learn a language. His advice: "Learn a little, use it a lot." Within one hour of your arrival at the work site, find a non-English speaker and speak to that person using at least one phrase from pre-trip language classes. If possible, enter into a short, basic conversation. Record your impressions from that conversation along with anything else that's on your heart.

# DAY TWO

Today's Date

Place

What I/we did today:

❖ ❖ ❖

## For Personal Devotion
*Being like Jesus.* (Read Philippians 2:5-11.)

## For Personal Reflection
One of the most significant aspects of the gospel is that Jesus became like us. How can you be like those you serve? There are numerous answers to that question. For example, consider the way you dress, the food you eat, the way you respond to situations, and even the thoughts you think. How are you using an incarnational approach to cross-cultural ministry?

## DAY THREE

Today's Date

Place

What I/we did today:

❖  ❖  ❖

### For Personal Devotion
*I became all things to all people.* (Read 1 Corinthians 9:19-23.)

### For Personal Reflection
Dr. Brewster classifies cross-cultural venturers in three ways: tourist, adventurer, and explorer. The tourist keeps his or her distance and observes the new experiences as an outsider. The adventurer jumps in with both feet and tries to experience every new thing. The explorer is like the adventurer but is not satisfied until he or she has broken new ground. Which are you? Do you approach cross-cultural travel like you thought you would? (Keep this question in mind during the rest of the week.)

## DAY FOUR

Today's Date

Place

What I/we did today:

❖   ❖   ❖

### For Personal Devotion
*Jonah's flight from right.* (Read the book of Jonah.)

### For Personal Reflection
Get to know one missionary within four days of arrival. Sit down with, or work alongside, the missionary and ask about his or her testimony, decision to become a missionary, life on the mission field, and plans for the future. Record the answers and your impressions here.

## DAY FIVE

Today's Date

Place

What I/we did today:

❖   ❖   ❖

### For Personal Devotion
*I am your servant.* (Read John 13:1-17.)

### For Personal Reflection
How are things going in my relationship with my team members? What are the struggles? Why do they exist? Do they have to do with the person, the mission trip, or the bombardment of emotions we feel? What constructive steps am I taking toward resolving the problems? Am I seeing strengths that I never knew existed in one of my friends on the trip? Have I told him or her?

## DAY SIX

Today's Date

Place

What I/we did today:

❖   ❖   ❖

**For Personal Devotion**
*The first short-term missionaries.* (Read Matthew 10:26-32.)

**For Personal Reflection**
Think about a conversation you have had with someone who lived in a foreign culture. Or, think about a book you may have read that deals with a missionary's encounter with a new culture. Do you recall any of the issues that person dealt with? Are you confronting those issues now? Consider what this trip would be like if you were alone and not part of a group. What if this were the first week of several years in this culture?

---

## DAY SEVEN

Today's Date

Place

What I/we did today:

❖   ❖   ❖

**For Personal Devotion**
*We're all parts of one Body.* (Read 1 Corinthians 12:12-31.)

**For Personal Reflection**
Which spiritual gifts are emerging or being reinforced in me as a result of my participation on this team?

---

## DAY EIGHT

Today's Date

Place

What I/we did today:

❖   ❖   ❖

**For Personal Devotion**
*Part of the team.* (Read 1 Corinthians 3:5-11.)

**For Personal Reflection**
How do you feel knowing that you are just a part of God's larger plan?
Does it make you feel insignificant? Why is your part important?

## DAY NINE

Today's Date

Place

What I/we did today:

❖ ❖ ❖

**For Personal Devotion**
*God cares for the oppressed.* (Read Psalm 10.)

**For Personal Reflection**
Have you seen oppression here? Does God seem to stand far off, or does He see the trouble and the grief?

## DAY TEN

Today's Date

Place

What I/we did today:

❖   ❖   ❖

**For Personal Devotion**
*Too busy with "service"?* (Read Luke 10:38-42.)

**For Personal Reflection**
Is it possible to be too busy doing "the Lord's work" to have time for God?
Are you doing that now on this trip? Do you do so at home?

## DAY ELEVEN

Today's Date

Place

What I/we did today:

❖ ❖ ❖

**For Personal Devotion**
*Giving your all.* (Read Luke 21:1-4.)

**For Personal Reflection**
In what ways have you seen people giving to God their "last two copper coins"?

## DAY TWELVE

Today's Date

Place

What I/we did today:

❖   ❖   ❖

**For Personal Devotion**
*The wicked and the pure.* (Read Psalm 73.)

**For Personal Reflection**
Do you get angry that the "wicked" prosper, while the "pure" suffer? Do you feel confused? Have you learned anything on this trip that helps you grapple with this difficult issue?

## DAY THIRTEEN

Today's Date

Place

What I/we did today:

❖   ❖   ❖

**For Personal Devotion**
*How will they know, if no one shows them?* (Read Acts 8:26-40.)

**For Personal Reflection**
During the past several days you have probably thought about ways to continue your involvement with Third-World Christians, or with the poor at home. You may want to tell others about God's power to work in the world and in people's lives. Resolve now to take at least one substantive step toward blending this past week's experiences with your future commitments and convictions.

## DAY FOURTEEN

Today's Date

Place

What I/we did today:

❖ ❖ ❖

**For Personal Devotion**
*Bless the Lord, O my soul!* (Read Psalm 103.)

**For Personal Reflection**
Tomorrow you will be home. During the past days you have been confronted by a variety of new sights, tastes, ideas, etc. Make a list below of the moments, the experiences, and the revelations that you want to be sure never to forget.

# VWAP CHECKLIST

This checklist is to be used by the planning committee and the team leader(s) as a guideline for the planning, coordinating, and implementing of a VWAP. Please refer to this checklist frequently and check off the items as they are completed.

## SIX MONTHS PRIOR TO DEPARTURE

❏ Establish planning committee.
❏ Explore possible destinations with selected agencies (see chapter 7, pages 49-51).
❏ Confirm location (this includes project, R & R portion, lodging, ground transportation).
❏ Contact travel agency or airline regarding flight arrangements and price (if traveling with ten or more, ask for group fares).
❏ Check into necessary documentation for travel to country.
❏ Check into necessary shots and preventive medication.
❏ Plan tentative itinerary.
❏ Order team member books.
❏ Select team leader(s).

## FOURTEEN WEEKS PRIOR TO DEPARTURE

❏ Establish a budget.
❏ Establish a per person price.
❏ Set payment dates.
❏ Design and produce promotion material.
❏ Begin promoting the team.
❏ Schedule announcement in church bulletin and classes.
❏ Distribute applications and give deadline for applications.
❏ Schedule information meeting.
❏ Contact church treasurer regarding handling of funds.

## TWELVE WEEKS PRIOR TO DEPARTURE

❑ Have information meeting.
❑ Begin collecting applications and deposits.
❑ Conduct interviews and check references.
❑ Schedule team preparation sessions and select location for meetings.
❑ Schedule commissioning service with church.

## TEN WEEKS PRIOR TO DEPARTURE

❑ Select team.
❑ Inform team members of team preparation meetings.
❑ Contact potential speaker/trainers for team preparation sessions.
❑ Plan fund-raising ideas.

## EIGHT WEEKS PRIOR TO DEPARTURE

❑ Reconfirm with mission agency and/or host community the size of team and any special arrangements.
❑ Have first team meeting to do the following.
  ❑ Review policy sheet.
  ❑ Discuss necessary documentation.
  ❑ Cover financial obligations/fund-raising.
❑ Confirm with travel agent and/or airline exact number of participants.

## SIX WEEKS PRIOR TO DEPARTURE

❑ Have second team meeting.
  ❑ Discuss medical requirements.
  ❑ Handle special medical requirements.
  ❑ Discuss fund-raising letters.
  ❑ Confirm passport applications.
  ❑ Pass out team roster with addresses and phone numbers.
❑ Get emergency contact phone number in country.

## FOUR WEEKS PRIOR TO DEPARTURE

❑ Have third team meeting.
  ❑ Formalize plans for collection drives.
  ❑ Assign team member responsibilities.
❑ Begin identifying people who will pray for team members using prayer partner forms.

## THREE WEEKS PRIOR TO DEPARTURE

❑ Have fourth team meeting.
  ❑ Discuss packing list.

❏ Review packing tips.
❏ Collect release of liability forms.
❏ Check on team members' finances.
❏ Collect prayer partner sheets.
❏ Encourage team members who buy new shoes to begin breaking them in to avoid blisters.
❏ Contact church treasurer regarding the procedure for obtaining necessary cash for team trip.
❏ Put together medical kit.

## TWO WEEKS PRIOR TO DEPARTURE

❏ Have the fifth team meeting.
  ❏ Review importance of journaling.
  ❏ Check on team finances.
  ❏ Check on necessary documentation and ask team members to make one copy.
  ❏ Schedule post-trip follow-up meetings.
  ❏ Schedule post-trip team presentation for congregation.
❏ Arrange for team transportation to and from airport.
❏ Purchase any necessary supplies.

## ONE WEEK PRIOR TO DEPARTURE

❏ Have final team meeting.
  ❏ Inform group of time and meeting place for flight.
  ❏ Collect final payment.
  ❏ Pass out emergency number.
  ❏ Pass out flight itinerary for team.
  ❏ Distribute any items team members need to pack.
  ❏ Collect copies of passports.
❏ Leave emergency numbers at church office.
❏ Obtain travelers' checks and church check for travel.
❏ Have team commissioning service.
❏ Reconfirm travel details with contact in country.

## ON-FIELD CHECKLIST

Review this checklist at least three days before the team's departure from home and/or at least one day before departure from the host community. As you complete each of the items, check them off. Then review this early on the day of the team's departure.

❏ Reconfirm team's flight reservations with the airlines from forty-eight to seventy-two hours prior to departure time.
❏ Discuss distribution of items (e.g., shoes, clothing, flashlights, etc.) the

team will be leaving behind with the missionary or the church pastor.

❏ Review the "Saying Good-By" section (pages 149-150) with the team on the day before good-bys will be said.

❏ Confirm transportation and arrangements for R & R portion.

❏ Confirm transportation to the airport on day of departure. Be at the airport at least two hours prior to departure for an international flight.

# PART SEVEN
# FORMS

*Conditional permission is given to copy pages 206-218 in this section for use with your VWAP team. You may copy the following pages for each team you lead. No pages in any other part of the book may be copied, nor may the following pages in this part be copied for any reason other than actual VWAP preparation.*

# VWAP TEAM APPLICATION

**Team Destination** _____

**Dates of Trip** _____

## PERSONAL INFORMATION

1. Name: _____

   Address: _____

   City: _____ State (Province): _____

   Zip: _____ Phone number: (_____)_____

2. Place of employment: _____

   Address: _____

   City: _____ State (Province): _____

   Zip: _____ Phone number: (_____)_____

   Job title: _____

3. Date of birth: _____ Place of birth: _____

4. Marital status:  ❑ Single ❑ Married

5. Passport number: _____

6. In the event of emergency, notify:

   Name: _____ Relationship: _____

   Address: _____

   City: _____ State (Province): _____ Zip: _____

   Day phone: (_____)_____ Evening phone: (_____)_____

7. Do you have any medical restrictions or handicaps that we need to make provision for?  ❑ No  ❑ Yes   If yes, explain:




8. Are you presently taking any medication?  ❑ No  ❑ Yes   If yes, explain:




9. Health insurance company: _____

   Policy number: _____

10. Physician name: _____

    Phone number: (_____)_____

## SKILLS

11. Please list any skills you have in languages other than English.




12. Check any of the skills below that apply to you. Give further explanation if necessary.

**Medical**
❑ Doctor
❑ Nurse
❑ Dentistry
❑ Nutrition
❑ Other (name it):

**Computer**
❑ Programming
❑ Data entry
❑ Word processing
❑ Other (name it):
List type of computer:

**Personal Ministry**
❑ Bible study leader
❑ Evangelism
❑ Singing (soloist)
❑ Musical instrument
❑ Other (name it):

**Construction**
❑ Carpentry
❑ Masonry
❑ Plumbing
❑ Electrical
❑ Other (name it):

**Business**
❑ Accounting
❑ Management
❑ Marketing
❑ Other (name it):

**Other**
❑ Horticulture
❑ Agriculture
❑ Arts/crafts
❑ Food service
❑ Other (name it):


## PERSONAL PROFILE

On a separate sheet of paper write one or two paragraphs on each of the following.

- A description of your relationship with Jesus Christ.
- Why you want to be on a Vacations with a Purpose team.
- The realistic roadblocks that might keep you from going on a VWAP.
- Any short-term teams you have been on before.

# COST PER PERSON

## GROUP COSTS

Printing                                  $_____

Postage                                   $_____

Ground Transportation                     $_____

Lodging***                                $_____

Project Materials                         $_____

    Total Group Costs         $_____ (1)

    Number of Team Members      _____ (2)

Average Cost Per Team Member (1 ÷ 2)        $_____ (3)

## INDIVIDUAL COSTS

Airline*                                  $_____

All Meals**                               $_____

Lodging***                                $_____

Country Tax                               $_____

Touring Costs                             $_____

Mission Agency Fee                        $_____

    Total Individual Cost         $_____ (4)

    Total Per Person Cost (3 + 4)     $_____

*Check with airline; it is possible that one or more may fly free.
**Includes "project" and R & R portions.
***May be individual or group, depending on accommodations.

# VWAP TEAM ACCOUNTING FORM

Form Submitted By: _____ Home Phone: _____

Signature: _____

Dates and Location of Trip: _____

Beginning Balance: $ _____

Total Amount Spent: $ _____

Cash Returned: $ _____

| DATE | DESCRIPTION | RECEIPT: YES/NO? | LODGING | GAS | FOOD | MISCELLANEOUS TRAVEL | GENERAL EXPENSES |
|---|---|---|---|---|---|---|---|
| | | | | | | | |
| | | | | | | | |
| | | | | | | | |
| | | | | | | | |
| | | | | | | | |
| | | | | | | | |
| | | | | | | | |
| | | | | | | | |
| | | | | | | | |
| | | | | | | | |
| | TOTALS | | | | | | |

NOTE: Please record expenditures in proper column and show all amounts in dollars.

## PRAYER PARTNERS

Please fill in this form carefully, then make a copy available to your team leader. The team leader will give it to someone who has volunteered to pray for you while you're gone. When you return, you will be told who your prayer partner has been.

Name: _____

Address: _____

City: _____ State (Province): _____ Zip: _____

The country I am going to is _____

The dates of my trip are _____ to _____

❖  ❖  ❖

To my prayer partner,

    Thank you for making a commitment to pray for me regularly as I participate on a mission team. In order to help you pray for me, I have completed the following:

I am going on a mission trip because:

I hope to accomplish the following while on this mission trip:

I would especially appreciate your prayers for:

## RELEASE OF LIABILITY

Some hosting agencies and consultant groups have found it wise to ask each participant to sign a release of liability. Shown below is the form used by one group. (By including a copy of this form, we do not in any way represent ourselves to be qualified to give legal advice. Be sure to check with an attorney.)

❖ ❖ ❖

In signing this form, I, _____, agree not to hold _____, its officers, employees, or other agents liable for any injury, loss, damage, or accident that I might encounter while on one of their mission trips.

    I realize and acknowledge that my participation on a mission trip to a foreign country includes many risks and possible dangers. I am well aware that my travel to such a foreign country exposes me to such risks as accidents, disease, war, political unrest, injury from construction projects, and other calamities.

    I hereby assume any such risks that might result from my travel to a foreign country, and I unconditionally agree to hold _____, its officers, employees, or other agents blameless for any liability concerning my personal health and well-being, or any liability for my personal property that might be lost, damaged, or stolen while on a mission trip.

    I have carefully read the foregoing and I understand that my signature herein holds _____, its officers, employees, or other agents harmless for any liability for injury, damage, loss, accident, delay, or irregularity in schedule.

Signed _____ and dated this _____ day of _____, 19_____.

WITNESSED BY _____,

STATE OF _____,

COUNTY OF _____.

On this _____ day of _____, 19_____, before me personally appeared _____ to be known to be the person(s) who executed the above release, and acknowledged that _____ voluntarily executed same.

NOTARY PUBLIC

Date of expiration of Notary Commission

Notary Seal

## VWAP EVALUATIONS

We would greatly appreciate it if you would take time to fill out this evaluation. Your input is important to us for planning teams in the future. Thanks!

Name: _____

Address: _____

1. Was this your first short-term mission trip? If not, please list others.

2. a. What do you think is the most significant thing you learned on this trip?

   b. How did this come about (i.e., what experiences, people, etc., helped you learn this)?

3. How did this trip differ from other trips, outreach programs, "missions" endeavors, or ministries that you have been exposed to?

4. Evaluate your team in the following areas on a scale of 1 (poor) to 5 (excellent). Please elaborate on low ratings. If possible, make comments on all areas.

_____ Teamwork                    _____ Attitudes

_____ Preparation                 _____ Relationships

_____ Adventure                   _____ Leadership

_____ Communication               _____ Exposure to culture

_____ Work accomplished           _____ Team devotional times

_____ Exposure to missions        _____ Concern for host community

5. Please evaluate the leader(s)/facilitator(s) of your team.

6. What aspect of the pretrip preparation was most helpful?

7. How could you or the team have been better prepared?

8. What aspects of the trip did you enjoy the most?

9. What aspects did you like least?

10. What would be your suggestions/observations concerning improving future mission teams?

11. Would you recommend a trip to someone else? Why, or why not?

12. a. What commitment to world missions would you now make as a result of your experience? How might this commitment work itself out in your life?

   b. How could you be encouraged in this?

13. Describe some of the ways you feel you grew spiritually as a result of your participation in this VWAP experience.

Your team leader may have additional questions for you to add to your evaluation. Please list and answer them in the space below.

## TEAM ROSTER 1

Name: _____ Phone (H): _____

Address: _____ Phone (W): _____

_____

Special Skills: _____

Special Medical Info: _____

Emergency Contact—Name: _____

Relationship: _____ Phone(s): _____

Name: _____ Phone (H): _____

Address: _____ Phone (W): _____

_____

Special Skills: _____

Special Medical Info: _____

Emergency Contact—Name: _____

Relationship: _____ Phone(s): _____

Name: _____ Phone (H): _____

Address: _____ Phone (W): _____

_____

Special Skills: _____

Special Medical Info: _____

Emergency Contact—Name: _____

Relationship: _____ Phone(s): _____

Name: _____ Phone (H): _____

Address: _____ Phone (W): _____

_____

Special Skills: _____

Special Medical Info: _____

Emergency Contact—Name: _____

Relationship: _____ Phone(s): _____

## TEAM ROSTER 2

In some countries, you may be required to give each person's name and passport number at certain checkpoints. Have several copies of this form available for such cases.

Full Name: _____ Passport #: _____

Full Name: _____ Passport #: _____

Full Name: _____ Passport #: _____

Full Name: _____ Passport #: _____

Full Name: _____ Passport #: _____

Full Name: _____ Passport #: _____

Full Name: _____ Passport #: _____

Full Name: _____ Passport #: _____

Full Name: _____ Passport #: _____

Full Name: _____ Passport #: _____

Full Name: _____ Passport #: _____

Full Name: _____ Passport #: _____

Full Name: _____ Passport #: _____

Full Name: _____ Passport #: _____

Full Name: _____ Passport #: _____

Full Name: _____ Passport #: _____

Full Name: _____ Passport #: _____

Full Name: _____ Passport #: _____

Full Name: _____ Passport #: _____

Full Name: _____ Passport #: _____

Full Name: _____ Passport #: _____

Full Name: _____ Passport #: _____

Full Name: _____ Passport #: _____

Full Name: _____ Passport #: _____

Full Name: _____ Passport #: _____

Full Name: _____ Passport #: _____

Full Name: _____ Passport #: _____

# RECOMMENDED READING LIST

Borthwick, Paul. *A Mind for Missions*. Colorado Springs, CO: NavPress, 1987.

Campolo, Anthony. *Who Switched the Price Tags?* Waco, TX: Word Books, 1986.

Engel, James F., and Jerry D. Jones. *Baby Boomers and the Future of World Missions*. Management Development Associates, 1989.

Hawthorne, Steven, and Ralph D. Winter, eds. *Perspectives on the World Christian Movement*. Pasadena, CA: William Carey Library, 1981.

Johnstone, Patrick. *Operation World*. Pasadena, CA: STL Books, 1986.

Kane, Herbert J. *Wanted: World Christians*. Grand Rapids, MI: Baker Book House, 1986.

Lappe, Frances Moore. *World Hunger: Twelve Myths*. New York: Grove Press, 1986.

Larson, Bruce. *Faith for the Journey*. Old Tappan, NJ: Fleming H. Revell Co., 1982.

Nash, Ronald H. *Liberation Theology*. Grand Rapids, MI: Baker Book House, 1988.

Sider, Ron. *Rich Christians in an Age of Hunger*. Downers Grove, IL: Inter-Varsity Press, 1977.

Sine, Tom. *The Mustard Seed Conspiracy*. Waco, TX: Word Books, 1981.

Sine, Tom. *Why Settle for More and Miss the Best?* Waco, TX: Word Books, 1987.

*Stepping Out: A Guide to Short-Term Missions*. Short-Term Missions Advocates, Inc., 1987 (P.O. Box 6018, Evanston, IL 60204).

Tremblay, Helene. *Families of the World: Family Life at the Close of the 20th Century (The Americas & The Caribbean).* New York: Farrar, Straus and Giroux, 1988.

Warner, David, trans. *Where There Is No Doctor.* Palo Alto, CA: Hisperian Foundation, 1977.

# More
# Resources
# for Your
# Ministry with
# Single Adults

Contact Singles Ministry Resources
for a FREE catalog of all the best resources available
to help you build an effective ministry
with single adults in your church
and community.

**Singles Ministry Resources**
P.O. Box 62056
Colorado Springs, Colorado  80962-2056

Or call (800) 487-4-SAM
or (719) 488-2610